A REFORMED CATHOLIC

A REFORMED CATHOLIC

A declaration, showing how near we may come to the present church of Rome in sundry points of religion and wherein we must forever depart from them, with an advertisement to all favorers of the Roman religion, showing that the said religion is against the catholic principles and grounds of the catechism

BY WILLIAM PERKINS

With an Introduction by Joseph A. Pipa

Published by Canon Press
P.O. Box 8729, Moscow, Idaho 83843
800.488.2034 | www.canonpress.com

William Perkins, *A Reformed Catholic*

First published in 1598.
Taken by permission from *The Works of William Perkins*, Vol. 7, Reformed Heritage Books, copyright ©2019.

Cover design by James Engerbretson
Cover illustration by Forrest Dickison
Interior design by Valerie Anne Bost and James Engerbretson

Printed in the United States of America.

Perkins, William, 1558-1602, author.
A reformed Catholic / by William Perkins ; with an introduction by Joseph A. Pipa, Jr.
Moscow, Idaho : Canon Press, 2021. | Series: Christian heritage series | "First published in 1598. Taken by permission from The Works of William Perkins, Vol. 7, Reformed Heritage Books, copyright 2019."
LCCN 2021019740 | ISBN 9781952410598 (paperback)
LCSH: Catholic Church—Controversial literature. | Catholic Church—Doctrines. | Reformed Church—Doctrines. | Protestant churches—Doctrines. | Catholic Church—Relations—Protestant churches. | Protestant churches—Relations—Catholic Church.
Classification: LCC BX1765.3 .P47 2021 | DDC 230/.42—dc23
LC record available at https://lccn.loc.gov/2021019740

20 21 22 23 24 25 10 9 8 7 6 5 4 3 2 1

CONTENTS

INTRODUCTION BY JOSEPH A. PIPA i

Dedication to Sir William Bowes 1

The author to the Christian reader 3

Revelation 18:4 5

The Places of Doctrine Handled

1. Of Free-will 11

2. Of Original Sin 21

3. Assurance of Salvation 27

4. Justification of a Sinner 41

5. Of Merits 65

6. Satisfaction for Sin 75

7. Of Traditions 85

8. Of Vows 95

9. Of Images 107

10. Of Real-presence 117

11. The Sacrifice of the Mass 129

12. Of Fasting 139

13. The State of Perfection 147

14. Worshipping of Saints Departed 155

15. Intercession of Saints 163

16. Implicit Faith 169

17. Of Purgatory 177

18. Of the Supremacy 181

19. Of the Efficacy of the Sacraments 189

20. Of Faith 195

21. Of Repentance 203

Advertisement to all Favorers of the Roman Religion 225

INTRODUCTION

William Perkins' *A Reformed Catholic* is as timely today as it was when he published it in 1597. Many evangelical Christians recognize little difference between Roman Catholicism and Evangelicalism. After all, the Roman Catholics hold to the Apostles' Creed and accept the Bible as the Word of God. We have often stood shoulder to shoulder with them in the battle against abortion. At the end of the day, we all are Christians and that is what matters. Is that conclusion valid? Many protestants in Elizabethan England were equally confused about Roman Catholicism.

Perkins wrote this book as an apologetic for Reformed (Reformation) Christianity to demonstrate that Reformed Protestantism was not a new religion, but the corrected progression of the Ancient Church. He desired to prove that English Protestantism was clearly in line with what the church had confessed and that it was the Roman Catholic church that had departed. He states his thesis in the title: "A Reformed Catholic or A Declaration Showing how near we may come to the present Church of Rome in Sundry points of Religion, and wherein we must forever depart from them, With an Advertisement to all favorers of the Roman religion, showing that the said religion is against the catholic principles and grounds of the catechism."

Some will object that such a book is not necessary today, after Vatican II. Vatican II changed the Roman Catholic church, and she is not what she once was. Admittedly, there are liberalizing tendencies in the Roman church, but she is as committed to the doctrines of the Council of Trent as she was in the sixteenth century.[1]

In this introduction, I will give some biographical information on Perkins and the circumstances in which he wrote, as well as an overview of the treatise.

William Perkins: The Man and His Times

Little is known about the early life of William Perkins. He was born in 1558 to Thomas and Anna Perkins in the village of Marston Jabbett, in Bulkington Parish of the county of Warwickshire. Since he enrolled as a pensioner at Christ's College, we may assume his family was fairly well to do;[2] and, more than likely, they had Puritan sympathies, as Christ's College was known for having many Puritan teachers.

He enrolled, June 1577, at Christ's College, Cambridge and studied under the famous Puritan Laurence Chaderton, who became his lifelong friend.[3] He remained in Cambridge all his life, taking a B.A. in 1581 and an M.A. in 1584. At this time,

---

1. The Council of Trent was the product of the Roman Catholic counter-reformation. It met in Trent (Trento), Italy from 1545 to 1563. It produced the irreducible doctrines of the Roman Catholic church.

2. A pensioner was a student at Cambridge who paid his expenses out of pocket.

3. Ian Breward, *The Works of William Perkins,* vol. 2 of the *Courtenay Library of Reformation Classics* (Berkshire: Sutton Courtenay Press, 1970), 3.

he was elected a fellow at Christ's College[4] and was ordained and appointed Lecturer[5] at Great St. Andrews, an important church across the street from Christ's College.

Like Calvin before him, he left no record of the occasion and circumstances of his conversion. Before his conversion, he was a profligate. Legend has it that he was a terrible drunkard. Supposedly, he overheard a woman tell her child, "Hold your tongue or I will give you to drunken Perkins yonder."[6] Although this story is probably apocryphal, Fuller relates that he was a wild young man when he went up to the University: "Quickly the wild fire of his youth began to break out... It is not certain whether his own disposition, or the bad company of others betrayed him to these extravagancies. Sure it is that he took such wild liberties to himself at cost of many a sigh in his reduced age. Probably divine providence permitted him to run himself with the prodigal son out of breath, that he might be the better enabled experimentally to reprove others of their vanity, effectually sympathising with their sad condition, and be the better skilled how to counsel and comfort them on their repentance. Why should God's arm, which afterwards graciously overtook Master Perkins, be too short to reach others in the same condition?"[7]

---

4. Thomas Fuller, *The Holy State and the Profane State,* 2 vols. (New York, 1938), 1:80. A fellow was a man appointed to tutor and teach students at one of the Colleges.

5. A lecturer was one called by a congregation or a group within a certain area to work alongside the local vicar or rector. An excellent discussion of the lectureships is Paul Seaver's *The Puritan Lectureships: The Politics of Religious Dissent 1560-1662* (Palo Alto, CA: Stanford University Press, 1970).

6. Benjamin Brook, *The Lives of the Puritans,* 3 vols. (1813; Morgan [PA]: Soli Deo Gloria Publications, 1994), 2:129.

7. Thomas Fuller, *Abel Redivivus: or the Dead Yet Speaking*, 2 vols. (London: William Tegg, 1867), 2:145-6.

From his own pen we learn that before his conversion Perkins was enthralled with black magic and the occult. He wrote in his *Resolution to the Country-man*, "I have long studied this Art, and was never quiet until I had seene all the secrets of the same: but at the length, it pleased God to lay before me the profannesse of it, may, I dare boldly say, Idolatrie, although it be covered with faire and golden shewes."[8]

Apparently, he was converted between 1581 and 1584, because by 1584 he was preaching to the prisoners at Cambridge Castle. Perkins was a powerful and faithful preacher able to reach all types of people in every social class. It was to the work of preaching that Perkins devoted his greatest energy. A good portion of his written works were developed from his sermons and expository lectures given at Great St. Andrews. Emerson gives two illustrations: "For instance, Perkins' commentary on Galatians was, its editor tells us, the substance of the Sunday lectures of three years. Similarly, Perkins' famous *Discourse of the Damned Art of Witchcraft* was first preached as a sermon."[9]

In addition to being a popular preacher, he was also an excellent scholar. As biographer T.T. Meril notes:

> He was a learned man. Thomas Fuller, his first notable biographer, claimed for him "a rare felicity in speedy reading of books, and as it were but turning them over would give an exact account of all considerables therein." [II 88-93] His most valuable characteristic, however, was his practical common sense which he exercised in everything he put his mind to. Better than any man of his age, he could

8. William Perkins, *Works,* vols 1 and 2 bound together (Cambridge: John Legatt, 1613), 2:653.

9. Everett Emerson, *English Puritanism from John Hooper to John Milton* (Durham: Duke University Press, 1968), 155-6.

> reduce the complexities of abstruse theological doctrine to simple counsel and simple language.[10]

The scope of his reading was so wide that, unlike some of his contemporaries who were criticized for only knowing modern writers, he was a profound student of the Church Fathers.[11] He also knew the classical writers and philosophers quite well. Through the pulpit and lecture hall, he influenced a prodigious number of Puritan luminaries who were influential preachers and theologians in the seventeenth century: Richard Sibbes, John Cotton, John Preston, and William Ames, to name but a few.

His consuming passion was pastoral reform. Breward describes Perkins' agenda: "He was deeply concerned at the lack of reformation amongst the common people, even compared with earlier in Elizabeth's reign. 'We are not now that which we have been twenty or thirty years ago. For now we see the world abounds with atheists, epicures, libertines, worldlings, neuters that are of no religion.' In light of this and the ever-present threat from Rome, Perkins set himself the task of meeting the religious needs of the time."[12]

Perkins was well equipped for this task. In addition to being a profound theologian, he was a popularizer and communicator par excellence. Moreover, he thought strategically. Early on, he grasped the importance of the printing press and, as noted above, by careful editing, he and his subsequent editors turned his sermons into books. In my opinion, he is one of the easiest Puritans to read.

---

10. T. T. Merril, ed. *William Perkins* (Nieuwkoop: B. De Graff, 1966), ix.

11. Emerson, 155.

12. Breward, 1970, 22.

Breward states that he became the most widely read Elizabethan theologian: "William Perkins of Cambridge was the most widely known theologian of the Elizabethan church. By the end of the sixteenth [century] he had replaced Calvin and Beza near the top of the English best-seller list. Even more important, his works were widely published outside Britain. At least fifty editions of Perkins' works were printed in Switzerland, the same number in various parts of Germany, almost ninety in the Netherlands, with smaller printings in France, Bohemia, Ireland, Hungary, plus translations into Spanish and Welsh published in London."[13]

In 1595, Perkins resigned his fellowship to marry Timothye Cradocke, a widow from the small village of Grantchester just outside of Cambridge.[14] They had seven children, three of whom died in childhood and one who was born after Perkins's death.

Perkins died on October 22, 1602, after several weeks of an intense attack of "stones."[15] On October 25, James Montague, later Bishop of Winchester, preached his funeral sermon on Joshua 1:2: "Moses My Servant Is Dead."[16] He was buried at the expense of Christ's College in the church yard of Great St. Andrews. [17]

In his methodology, Muller places him in the early phase of the first period of Reformed Orthodoxy.[18] These are the

---

13. Breward, 1970, xi.

14. Fellows were not allowed to be married.

15. More than likely gallstones.

16. Fuller 1938, 1:82.

17. Emerson, 159.

18. Richard Muller, *Post-Reformation Reformed Dogmatics: The Rise and Development of Reformed Orthodoxy, ca. 1520 to ca. 1725*, 4 vols. 2nd ed (Grand Rapids: Baker Academic, 2003), 1, 31.

men who systematically organized the doctrines of Scripture. (One might say they were the first systematic theologians.) Building on an exegetical foundation, they used the methods of the schools (universities) to organize their material. Muller describes their methodology:

> It is a theology designed to develop system on a highly technical level and in an extremely precise manner by means of the careful identification of topics, division of these topics into their basic parts, definition of the parts, and doctrinal or logical argumentation concerning the divisions and definitions. This, moreover (sic) is the sense of the term used by the writers of the sixteenth century to describe their own academic, technical, and disputative theology as distinct from other genre and approaches, namely, the catechetical, biblical-exegetical, and simply didactic or ecclesial.[19]

His commitment to the methods of Reformed Scholasticism equipped him to be an effective polemical writer, as seen in this treatise. He, however, never lost sight of the need to wed theology with piety.[20] He defined theology as "the science of living blessedly forever."[21]

Why this book? To understand the times, we need to remember what Britain was like ecclesiastically when Elizabeth came to the throne. Elizabeth's father, Henry VIII, separated the English church from Rome in 1534. From then until his death in 1547, the church was in constant turmoil. During the

19. Muller, 34, 35. Perhaps the best way to understand the method is that in a systematic theology book each *loci* of doctrine is drawn from Scripture in a logical order. The other genres would have been catechisms, commentaries and sermons, practical, devotional, and polemical books.

20. Breward, xi.

21. Perkins, *Golden Chain*, vol. 6, 1.11.

eleven years between the death of Henry VIII and Elizabeth's coming to the throne, the church became Protestant under Edward VI, and then Roman Catholic under Mary Tudor. Religious chaos and turmoil were the order of the day. The people were biblically illiterate, and there were few able preachers to remedy the problem.

Perkins and his fellow Puritans were greatly concerned about the scarcity of preachers. Although there was some improvement during the reign of Elizabeth, things remained bleak in Perkins' day. Breward states: "He [Perkins] stood within a long tradition of complaint at this point [lack of able preachers]. Tyndale had wanted all clergy to be able and conscientious preachers, but by 1583 only one sixth of the English clergy were licensed to preach. After a strenuous campaign by Whitgift to raise the standards of the clergy, there were still only 4,830 licensed to preach in 1603. There were 9,244 parishes."[22]

Politically and ecclesiastically, when Elizabeth ascended the throne in 1558, she faced enormous difficulties. The Roman Catholics declared her illegitimate and not a true heir to the throne. Her sister Mary's attempt to rule had been disastrous and thus many were opposed to a female ruler. The church was in chaos and many of Elizabeth's subjects did not know what the true church was.

The situation was exacerbated by the constant attempts of Rome to overthrow Elizabeth and put Mary, Queen of Scots, on the throne. There were several plots to assassinate Elizabeth.[23] In 1570, the Pope excommunicated her and encour-

22. Perkins, 35.

23. Shawn D. Wright and Andrew S. Ballitch eds., *The Works of William Perkins*, vol. 7 (Grand Rapids: Reformation Heritage Books, 2019), xx.

aged the people to rebel.[24] There was also the notorious failed attempt of the Spanish Armada to invade England and put a papist on the throne.

But more serious in the long run were the attempts to proselytize and turn the people to Romanism. In the early years of Elizabeth's reign, over one hundred men committed to the papacy fled from Oxford to the continent, many of whom trained to become priests.[25] In 1568, a seminary was established in Douai and another in Rome in 1576 to train young English priests and send them surreptitiously into England.[26] Throughout the reign of Elizabeth, there remained a group of confirmed Romanists called Recusants. The priests would sneak into England to distribute literature and say Masses on private estates, many of which had "priest holes," where the priests were hidden. Because the common people had been so poorly taught, they were easily beguiled by these men. Many could discern little difference between Romanism and Protestantism.

This halting between two opinions greatly distressed Perkins. In his commentary on Galatians, he alludes to certain men who were Protestants in England, while in other countries attended Mass, describing them as men "who change their religion with the times."[27] It was in this context that Perkins wrote *A Reformed Catholic*. As I wrote above, his title is the thesis: "A Reformed Catholic or A Declaration Showing how near we may come to the present Church of Rome in

---

24. Wright and Ballitch, xx.

25. Wright and Ballitch, xx.

26. W.H. Frere, *The English Church in the Reigns of Elizabeth and James I. (1558-1625)* (London: Macmillan and Co., Limited, 1904), 207.

27. William Perkins, *The Works of William Perkins, vol.2*, ed. Paul M. Smalley (Grand Rapids: Reformation Heritage Books, 2015), 102.

Sundry points of Religion, and wherein we must forever depart from them, With an Advertisement to all favorers of the Roman religion, showing that the said religion is against the catholic principles and grounds of the catechism."[28]

In the address to the Christian reader, Perkins defines what he meant by the title: "By a Reformed Catholic, I understand anyone that holds the same necessary heads of religion with the Roman Church; yet so as he pares off and rejects all errors in doctrine whereby the said religion is corrupted."[29] He intended to demonstrate that the Reformed Church was the true Catholic Church and that Rome had departed from the essential doctrines of historic Christianity.

Perkins has a three-fold purpose: first, to confute the arguments of those who contended that the English protestant church and the Roman church differed "not in substance, and consequently that they may be reconciled;" second, that the papist might have a better understanding of the historic nature of English Protestantism; and third, that the common people would learn the errors of the Roman church.[30]

He begins with a brief exposition of Revelation 18:4: "And I heard another voice from heaven say, 'Go out of her, my people, that ye not be partakers of her sins, and receive not of her plagues.'" In developing the treatise, Perkins uses the format that he popularized for preaching: After a brief exposition of the text, he develops the doctrine which is then explained and demonstrated. [31]

28. Title page.

29. Page 3.

30. Ibid.

31. William Perkins, *Works,* vol. 10, ed. Joseph A. Pipa and J. Stephen Yuille (Grand Rapids: Reformation Heritage Books, 2020), 281-356.

Perkins interprets Babylon as the city of Rome with its empire and, by type, the papacy as the antichrist. The command to separate is spiritual, "as of a spiritual separation in respect of faith and religion."[32]

Perkins thus says he will defend the following doctrine: "Thus then, we see that the words contain a commandment from God enjoining His church and people to make a separation from Babylon. Whence I observe, that all those who will be saved, must depart and separate themselves from the faith and religion of this present Church of Rome."[33] He devotes the remainder of the book to prove this doctrine.

The main section of the treatise enumerates twenty-one doctrines and practices of the Roman church by which Perkins seeks to do two things: "First, how far forth we may join with them in the matter of religion. Second, how far forth and wherein we must dissent and depart from them." He generally follows this arrangement: our consent; the dissent or difference; our reasons; and the objections of papists, although at times he changes the order or conflates two headings into one.

In the second section, he details seven sins of the Roman Church. The conclusion of which is "to eschew all the sins of the Church of Rome, that they may withal escape her deserved plagues and punishments."[34]

After he discusses the sins of Rome, he adds an appendix: "An Advertisement to all Favorers of the Roman Religion, Showing that the said Religion is Against the Catholic Principles and Grounds of the Catechism."[35] In this brief section,

32. Page 12 of text in vol. 7 collected works.

33. Ibid., 12.

34. Perkins, vol. 7 collected works, 157.

35. By "catechism" he meant the apostolic and catholic confession of these doctrines.

he demonstrates that "the Roman religion now established by the Council of Trent, is in the principal points thereof against the very grounds of the Catechism that have been agreed upon ever since the days of the apostles, by all churches." He details four areas in which Rome had departed from the essential beliefs of historic Christianity: The Apostles' Creed, the Ten Commandments, the Lord's Prayer, and the Institution of the two sacraments: Baptism and the Lord's Supper.

His conclusion is pointed, but pastoral:

> These few lines, as also the former treatise, I offer to the view and reading of them that favor the Roman religion—willing them with patience to consider this one thing, that their religion, if it were catholic and apostolic (as they pretend), could not be contrary so much as in one point, to the grounds of all catechisms that have been used in Churches confessing the name of Christ ever since the apostles' days. And whereas it crosses the said grounds in sundry points of doctrine (as I have proved), it is a plain argument that the present Roman religion is degenerate. I write not this despising or hating their person for their religion, but wishing unfeignedly their conversion in the world, and their salvation in the world to come.[36]

It is my prayer that the Holy Spirit will use this edition of *A Reformed Catholic* to accomplish the author's purpose.

~Dr. Joseph A. Pipa

36. Last paragraph.

DEDICATION

To the right worshipful, Sir William Bowes, Knight, etc.

Grace and Peace

Right Worshipful, it is a notable policy of the devil, which he has put into the heads of sundry men in this age, to think that our religion, and the religion of the present Church of Rome are all one for substance; and that they may be re-united as (in their opinion) they were before. Writings to this effect are spread abroad in the French tongue, and respected of English Protestants more than is meet, or ought to be. For, let men in show of moderation pretend the peace and good estate of the Catholic Church as long as they will; this union of the two religions can never be made, more than the union of light and darkness. And this shall appear, if we do but a little consider, how they of the Roman church have razed the foundation. For though in words they honor Christ, yet in deed they turn Him into a pseudo-Christ and an idol of their own brain. They call Him our Lord; but with this condition, that the servant of servants of this Lord may change and add to His commandments, having so great a power that he may open and shut heaven to whom he will, and bind the very conscience with his own laws, and consequently be partaker of the spiritual kingdom of Christ. Again, they call Him a Savior, but yet in us—in that He gives this grace unto us, that by our merits we may be our own saviors, and in the want of our own merits we may partake in the merits of the saints. And they acknowledge that He died and suffered for us, but with this caveat, that the fault being pardoned we must satisfy for the temporal punishment either in this world or in purgatory. In a word, they make Him our Mediator of intercession unto God; but withal, His mother must be the queen of heaven, and by the right of a mother command Him there. Thus, in word they cry "Hosanna," but indeed they crucify Christ. Therefore, we have good cause to bless the name of God that has freed us from the yoke of this Roman bondage and has brought us to the true light and liberty of the gospel. And it should be a great height of unthankfulness in us, not to stand out against the present Church of Rome, but to yield ourselves to plots of reconciliation. To this effect and purpose, I have penned this little treatise, which I present to your worship, desiring it might be some token of a thankful mind for undeserved love. And I crave withal, not only your worshipful (which is more common) but also your learned protection; being well assured, that by skill and art you are able to justify whatsoever I have truly taught. Thus wishing to you and yours the continuance and the increase of faith and good conscience, I take my leave. Cambridge, June 28, 1597.

Your worship's in the Lord, William Perkins

THE AUTHOR TO THE CHRISTIAN READER

By a Reformed Catholic, I understand anyone that holds the same necessary heads of religion with the Roman Church; yet so as he pares off and rejects all errors in doctrine whereby the said religion is corrupted. How this may be done, I have begun to make some little declaration in this small treatise, the intent whereof is to show how near we may come to the present Church of Rome in sundry points of religion, and wherein we must ever dissent.

My purpose in penning this small treatise is threefold. The first is to confute all such politics as hold and maintain that our religion and that of the Roman Church differ not in substance, and consequently that they may be reconciled. Yet my meaning here is not to condemn any pacification that tends to persuade the Roman Church to our religion. The second is, that the papists which think so basely of our religion may be won to a better liking of it when they shall see how near we come unto them in sundry points. The third, that the common Protestant might in some part see and conceive the points of difference between us and the Church of Rome and know in what manner and how far forth we condemn the opinions of the said church.

I crave pardon for the order which I use in handling the several points. For I have set them down one by one, as they came to mind, not respecting the laws of method. If any papist shall say that I have not alleged their opinions aright, I answer that their books be at hand, and I can justify what I have said.

Thus craving your acceptation for this my pains, and wishing unto you the increase of knowledge and love of pure and sound religion, I take my leave and make an end.

REVELATION 18:4

And I heard another voice from heaven say, "Go out of her, my people, that ye not be partakers of her sins, and receive not of her plagues."

In the former chapter, Saint John sets down a description of the whore of Babylon, and that at large as he saw her in a vision described unto him. In the sixteenth verse of the same chapter, he foretells her destruction. And in the first three verses of this 18th chapter, he goes on to propound the said destruction yet more directly and plainly; withal alleging arguments to prove the same, in all the verses following. Now in this fourth verse is set down a caveat, serving to forewarn all the people of God, that they may escape the judgment which shall befall the whore. And the Word contains two parts: a commandment, and a reason. The commandment, "Come out of her, my people," that is, from Babylon. The reason, taken from the event "lest you be partakers, etc." Touching the commandment, first I will search the right meaning of it and then set down the use thereof and doctrine flowing thence. In history, therefore, are three Babylons mentioned: One is Babylon of Assyria standing on the river

Euphrates, where was the confusion of languages, and where the Jews were in captivity, which Babylon is, in Scripture, reproached for idolatry and other iniquities. The second Babylon is in Egypt, standing on the river Nile, and it is now called Cayr; of that mention is made in 1 Peter 5:13 (as some think) though indeed it is as likely and more commonly thought that there is meant Babylon of Assyria. The third Babylon is mystical, whereof Babylon of Assyria was a type and figure; and that is Rome, which is without question here to be understood. And the whore of Babylon, as by all circumstances may be gathered, is the state or regiment of a people that are the inhabitants of Rome and appertain thereto. This may be proved by the interpretation of the Holy Ghost, for in the last verse of the seventeenth chapter the woman, that is, the whore of Babylon, is said to be "a city which reigneth over the kings of the earth."[1]

Now in the days when Saint John penned this book of Revelation, there was no city in the world that ruled over the kings of the earth but Rome; it then being the seat where the emperor put in execution his imperial authority. Again, in the seventh verse she is said to "sit on a beast having seven heads and ten horns," which seven heads be "seven hills" (v. 9), whereon the woman sits; and also they be "seven kings." Therefore, by the whore of Babylon is meant a city standing on seven hills. Now it is well known, not only to learned men in the church of God, but even to the heathen themselves, that Rome alone is the city built on seven distinct hills, called Caelius, Aventinus, Exquilinus, Tarpeius (or Capitoline), Viminalis, Palatinus, Quirinalis. Papists, to help themselves, do allege that old Rome stood on seven hills, but now it is removed further to Campus Martius. I answer, that howsoever

1. This paragraph break is not in the original.

the greatest part of the city in regard of habitation be not now on seven hills, yet in regard of regiment and practice of religion it is; for even to this day upon these hills are seated certain churches and monasteries and other like places where the papal authority is put in execution. And thus, Rome being put for a state and regiment, even at this day it stands upon seven hills. And though it be come to pass that the harlot, in regard of her later days even changed her seat, yet in respect of her younger times in which she was bred and born, she sat upon the seven hills. Others, because they fear the wounding of their own heads, labor to frame these words to another meaning, and say that by the whore is meant the company of all wicked men in the world wheresoever, the devil being the head thereof. But this exposition is flat against the text—for in the second verse of the seventeenth chapter, she is opposed to the kings of the earth, with whom she is said to commit fornication. And in the last verse she is called a city standing on seven hills and reigning over the kings of the earth (as I have said), and therefore must needs be a state of men in some particular place. And the papists themselves, perceiving that this shift will not serve their turn, make two Romes: heathenish Rome, and that whereof the pope is head. Now (say they) the whore spoken of is heathenish Rome, which was ruled by cruel tyrants, as Nero, Domitian, and the rest, and that Rome whereof now the pope is head is not here meant. Behold a vain and foolish distinction, for ecclesiastical Rome in respect of state, princely dominion, and cruelty in persecuting the saints of God, is all one with the heathenish empire, the see of the bishop being turned into the emperor's court as all histories do manifest. But let the distinction be as they suppose, yet by their leave, here by the whore must be understood not only heathenish Rome, but even the papal or ecclesiastical Rome. For, [in] verse 3 of this chapter the Holy Ghost says plainly that she "hath made all nations drunk with the wine of the wrath of her fornication." Yes, it is added "that she hath committed fornication with the kings of the earth," whereby is signified that she has endeavored to entangle all the nations of the earth in her spiritual idolatry and to bring the kings of the earth to her religion. Which thing cannot be understood of heathenish Rome, for that left all the kings of the earth to their own religion and idolatry. Neither did they labor to bring foreign kings to worship their gods. Again, chapter 17, verse 16, it is said, "that the ten horns which be ten kings, shall hate the whore, and make her desolate and naked"; which must not be understood of heathenish Rome, but of popish Rome. For, whereas in former times, all the kings of the earth did submit themselves to the whore, now they have begun to withdraw themselves and make her desolate; as the king of Bohemia, Denmark, Germany, England, Scotland, and other parts. Therefore, this distinction is also frivolous. They further allege that the whore of Babylon is drunk with the blood of the saints and martyrs (chap. 17:6) shed not in Rome, but in Jerusalem, where "the Lord was crucified," and the two prophets being slain "lie there in the streets" (Rev. 11:8). But this place is not meant of Jerusalem, as Jerome has fully taught, but it may well be understood of Rome.[2] Christ was crucified there, either because the authority whereby He was crucified was from the Roman Empire, or else because Christ in His members was and is there daily crucified, though locally in His own person He was crucified at Jerusalem.[3]

And thus, notwithstanding all which has been said, we must here by the whore understand the state and empire of Rome,

2. In the margin: Epist. 17. Eusto. & Paulae: *ad Marcellam.*

3. This paragraph break is not in the original.

not so much under the heathen emperors as under the head thereof, the pope. Which exposition, besides the authority of the text, has the favor and defense of ancient and learned men. Bernard says, "They are the ministers of Christ, but they serve Antichrist".[4] Again, "The beast spoken of in the Apocalypse, to which a mouth is given to speak blasphemies, and to make war with the saints of God, is now gotten into Peter's chair, as a lion prepared to his prey."[5] It will be said that Bernard speaks these latter words of one that came to the popedom by intrusion or usurpation. It is true indeed, but wherefore was he a usurper? He renders a reason thereof in the same place—because the anti-pope called Innocentius was chosen by the kings of Almaine,[6] France, England, Scotland, Spain, Jerusalem, with consent of the whole clergy and people in these nations, and the other was not. And thus, Bernard has given his verdict, that not only this usurper, but all the popes for this many years, are the beasts in the Apocalypse, because now they are only chosen by the college of cardinals. To this agrees the decree of Pope Nicolas II, anno 1059, that the pope shall afterward be created by the suffrages of the cardinal bishops of Rome, with the consent of the rest of the clergy and people, and the emperor himself.[7] And all popes "are excommunicate and accursed as antichrists," that enter otherwise, as all now do [2 Thess. 2].[8] Joachimus Abbas says, "Antichrist was long since born in Rome, and shall be yet advanced higher in the apostolic see." Petrarch says, "Once Rome, now Babylon." And Irenaeus *lib.* 5, *cap.* last, said before all these, "that Antichrist should be *Lateinus*," a Roman.

---

4. In the margin: *Serm. in Can.* 33.
5. In the margin: *Epi.* 125.
6. *Almaine*: Germany.
7. In the margin: *c. in nomine dist.* 23
8. In the margin: *Referente Juello.*

Again, this commandment must not so much be understood of a bodily departure in respect of cohabitation and presence, as of a spiritual separation in respect of faith and religion. And the meaning of the Holy Ghost is that men must depart from the Romish Church in regard of judgment and doctrine, in regard of their faith and the worship of God.

Thus then, we see that the words contain a commandment from God, enjoining His church and people to make a separation from Babylon. Whence I observe, *that all those who will be saved, must depart and separate themselves from the faith and religion of this present Church of Rome.* And whereas they are charged with schism that separate on this manner; the truth is, they are not schismatics that do so because they have the commandment of God for their warrant. And that party is the schismatic in whom the cause of this separation lies; and that is in the Church of Rome, namely the cup of abomination in the whore's hand, which is their heretical and schismatic religion.

Now touching this duty of separation, I mean to speak at large, not standing so much to prove the same, because it is evident by the text, as to show the manner and measure of making this separation. And therein I will handle two things: First, how far forth we may join with them in the matter of religion. Second, how far forth and wherein we must dissent and depart from them. And for this cause, I mean to make choice of certain points of religion, and to speak of them in as good order as I can, showing in each of them our consent and difference. And the rather, because some harp much upon this string, that a union may be made of our two religions, and that we differ not in substance, but in points of circumstance.

The first point wherewith I mean to begin shall be the point of free will, though it be not the principal.

THE FIRST POINT

Of Free Will

I. Our Consent

Free will, both by them and us, is taken for a mixed power in the mind and will of man whereby, discerning what is good and what is evil, he accordingly chooses or refuses the same.

Conclusion 1. Man must be considered in a fourfold estate: as he was created, as he was corrupted, as he is renewed, as he shall be glorified. In the first estate, we ascribe to man's will liberty of nature in which he could will or nill either good or evil; in the third, liberty of grace; in the last, liberty of glory. All the doubt is of the second estate; and yet therein also we agree, as the conclusions following will declare.

Conclusion 2. The matters whereabout free will is occupied are principally the actions of men, which be of three sorts: natural, human, spiritual. Natural actions are such as are common to men with beasts, as to eat, drink, sleep, hear, see, smell, taste, and to move from place to place. In all which we join with the papists and hold that man has [a] free will, and ever since the fall of Adam, by a natural power of the mind, freely performs any of these actions or the like.

Conclusion 3. Human actions are such as are common to all men, good and bad, as to speak and use reason, the practice of all mechanical and liberal arts, and the outward performance of civil and ecclesiastical duties, as to come to the church, to speak and preach the Word, to reach out the hand to receive the sacrament, and to lend the ear to listen outwardly to that which is taught. And hither we may refer [to] the outward actions of civil virtues; as namely, justice, temperance, gentleness, liberality. And in these also we join with the Church of Rome and say (as experience teaches), that men have a natural freedom of will to put them, or not to put them, in execution. Paul says [in] Romans 2:14, "The Gentiles that have not the law, do the things of the law by nature," that is, by natural strength. And he says of himself, that before his conversion, touching the righteousness of the law, "he was unblameable" (Phil. 3:6). And for this external obedience, natural men receive reward in temporal things (Matt. 6:5; Ezek. 29:19). And yet here some caveats must be remembered: 1. That in human actions, man's will is weak and feeble and his understanding dim and dark; and thereupon he often fails in them. And in all such actions, with Augustine I understand the will of man to be only wounded or half dead. 2. That the will of man is under the will of God, and therefore to be ordered by it, as Jeremiah says in chapter 10:23, "O Lord I know that the way of man is not in himself. Neither is it in man to walk or direct his steps."

Conclusion 4. The third kind of actions are spiritual, more nearly concerning the heart or conscience, and these be twofold: They either concern the kingdom of darkness or else the kingdom of God. Those that concern the kingdom of darkness are sins properly, and in these we likewise join with the papists and teach that in sins or evil actions man has freedom of will. Some peradventure will say that we sin necessarily, because he that sins cannot but sin, and that free will and necessity cannot stand together. Indeed, the necessity of compulsion or co-action and free will cannot agree. But there is another kind of necessity which may stand with freedom of will, for some things may be done necessarily and also freely. A man that is in close prison must needs there abide and cannot possibly get forth and walk where he will; yet can he move himself freely and walk within the prison. So likewise, though man's will be chained naturally by the bond[s] of sin, and therefore cannot but sin, and thereupon sins necessarily, yet it also sins freely.

Conclusion 5. The second kind of spiritual actions or things concern the kingdom of God, as repentance, faith, the conversion of a sinner, new obedience, and such like, in which we likewise in part join with the Church of Rome and say that in the first conversion of a sinner, man's free will concurs with God's grace as a fellow or co-worker in some sort. For in the conversion of a sinner three things are required: the Word, God's Spirit, and man's will. For man's will is not passive in all and every respect but has an action in the best conversion and change of the soul. When any man is converted, this work of God is not done by compulsion, but he is converted willingly; and at the very time when he is converted, by God's grace He wills his conversion. To this end says Augustine, *Serm. 15 de verb. Apost.*, "He which made you without you, will not save you without you." Again, "That is certain, that our will is required in this, that we may do any good thing well. But we have it not from our own power, but God works to will in us."[1] For look at what time God gives grace, at thesame time He[2] gives a will to desire and will the same grace. As, for example, when God works faith, at the same time He

1. In the margin: *de grat. et lib. arbit.*1.

2. In the margin: *Posse velle, et actu velle recipere.*

works also upon the will, causing it to desire faith and willingly to receive the gift of believing. God makes of the unwilling will a willing will; because no man can receive grace utterly against his will, considering will constrained is no will. But here we must remember that howsoever, in respect of time, the working of grace by God's Spirit and the willing of it in man go together. Yet in regard of order, grace is first wrought, and man's will must first of all be acted and moved by grace, and then it also acts, wills, and moves itself. And this is the last point of consent between us and the Roman Church touching free will. Neither may we proceed further with them.

II. The Dissent or Difference

The point of difference stands in the cause of the freedom of man's will in spiritual matters, which concern the kingdom of God. The papists say man's will concurs and works with God's grace in the first conversion of a sinner, *by itself*, and by its own natural power, and is only helped by the Holy Ghost. We say that man's will works with grace in the first conversion, yet not of itself, but by grace. Or thus: They say will has a natural cooperation; we deny it and say it has cooperation only by grace, being in itself not active but passive, willing well only as it is moved by grace, whereby it must first be acted and moved before it can act or will. And that we may the better conceive the difference, I will use this comparison: The Church of Rome sets forth the estate of a sinner by the condition of a prisoner, and so do we. Mark then the difference. It supposes the said prisoner to lie bound hand and foot with chains and fetters and withal to be sick and weak, yet not wholly dead but living in part. It supposes also, that being in this case, he stirs not himself for any help, and yet has ability and power to stir. Hereupon, if the keeper come and take away his bolts and fetters and hold him by the hand and help him up, he can and will of himself stand and walk and go out of prison. "Even so," say they, "is a sinner bound hand and foot with the chain of his sins; and yet he is not dead but sick, like to the wounded man in the way between Jericho and Jerusalem. And therefore, he does not will and affect that which is good; but if the Holy Ghost come and do but untie his bands and reach him His hand of grace, then can he stand of himself and will his own salvation or anything else that is good." We, in like manner, grant that a prisoner fitly resembles a natural man, but yet such a prisoner must he be as is not only sick and weak but even stark dead; which cannot stir though the keeper untie his bolts and chains, nor hear though he sound a trumpet in his ear. And if the said keeper would have him to move and stir, he must give him not only his hand to help him, but even soul and life also. And such a one is every man by nature, not only chained and fettered in his sins, but stark dead therein, as one that lies rotting in the grave not having any ability or power to move or stir. And therefore, he cannot so much as desire or do anything that is truly good of himself. But God must first come and put a new soul into him, even the Spirit of grace to quicken and revive him. And then being thus revived, the will begins to will good things at the very same time when God by His Spirit first infuses grace. And this is the true difference between us and the Church of Rome in this point of free will.

III. Our Reasons

Now for the confirmation of the doctrine we hold, namely, that a man wills not his own conversion of himself by nature, either in whole or in part, but by grace wholly and alone, these reasons may be used:[3]

---

3. This paragraph break is not in the original.

Reason 1. The first is taken from the nature and measure of man's corruption, which may be distinguished into two parts: The first is the want of that original righteousness, which was in man by creation. The second is a proneness and inclination to that which is evil, and to nothing that is truly good. This appears, [in] Genesis 8:21, "The frame of man's heart (says the Lord,) is evil even from his childhood." That is, the disposition of the understanding, will, affections with all that the heart of man devises, forms, or imagines, is wholly evil. And Paul says, "The wisdom of the flesh is enmity against God" (Rom. 8:7), which words are very significant. For the word φρὸνημα, translated "wisdom," signifies that the best thoughts, the best desires, affections, and endeavors that be in any natural man—even those that come most near to true holiness—are not only contrary to God, but even enmity itself. And hence I gather, that the very heart itself, that is, the will and mind from whence these desires and thoughts do come, are also enmity unto God. For such as the action is, such is the faculty whence it proceeds; such as the fruit is, such is the tree; such as the branches are, such are the roots. By both these places it is evident that in man there is not only a want, absence, or deprivation of original righteousness, but a proneness also by nature unto that which is evil—which proneness includes in it an inclination not to some few, but to all and every sin, the very sin against the Holy Ghost not excepted. Hence therefore I reason thus:

> *If every man, by nature, does both want original justice and be also prone unto all evil, then wants he natural free will to will that which is truly good.*
> *But every man by nature wants original justice and is also prone unto all evil.*
> *Ergo: Every man naturally wants free will to will that which is good.*

Reason 2. "The natural man perceiveth not the things of the Spirit of God, for they are foolishness unto him; neither can he know them because they are spiritually discerned" (1 Cor. 2:14). In these words, Saint Paul sets down these points: 1. That a natural man does not so much as think of the things revealed in the gospel. 2. That a man hearing, and in mind conceiving them, cannot give consent unto them and by natural judgment approve of them, but contrariwise thinks them to be foolishness. 3. That no man can give assent to the things of God unless he be enlightened by the Spirit of God. And hence I reason thus:

> *If a man by nature does not know and perceive the things of God, and when he shall know them cannot by nature give assent unto them, then has he no power to will them.*
> *But the first is evidently true: Ergo.*

For first, the mind must approve and give assent before the will can choose or will, and when the mind has neither power to conceive nor give assent, there the will has no power to will.

Reason 3. Third, the Holy Ghost avouches that all men by nature are "dead in sins and trespasses" (Eph. 2:1; Col. 2:13), not as the papists say: weak, sick, or half dead. Hence, I gather that man wants natural power not to will simply, but freely and frankly to will that which is truly good. A dead man in his grave cannot stir the least finger because he wants the very power of life, sense, and motion. No more can he that is dead in sin will the least good. No, if he could either will or do any good, he could not be dead in sin. And as a dead man in the grave cannot rise but by the power of God, no more can he that is dead in sin rise but by the power of God's grace alone without any power of his own.

Reason 4. Fourth, in the conversion and salvation of a sinner, the Scripture ascribes all to God and nothing to man's free will. "Except a man be born again, he cannot see the kingdom of God" (John 3:3). "We are his workmanship created in Christ Jesus to good works" (Eph. 2:10). And, [in Eph.] *ch.* 4, *v.* 24, "The new man is created in the image of God." Now to be born again is a work of no less importance than our first creation, and therefore wholly to be ascribed to God as our creation is. Indeed, Paul, in Philippians 2:12–13, bids the Philippians [to] "work out their salvation with fear and trembling," not meaning to ascribe unto them a power of doing good by themselves. And therefore, in the next verse, he adds, "It is God that worketh both the will and the deed," directly excluding all natural free will in things spiritual. And yet, withal, he acknowledges that man's will has a work in doing that which is good—not by nature, but by grace—because when God gives man [the] power to will good things, then he can will them; and when He gives him a power to do good, then he can do good, and he does it. For though there be not in man's conversion a natural cooperation of his will with God's Spirit, yet is there a supernatural cooperation by grace, enabling man, when he is to be converted, to will his conversion. According to which, Saint Paul says, "I have labored in the faith" (1 Cor. 15:10). But lest any man should imagine that this was done by any natural power, therefore he adds, "yet not I," that is, not I by anything in me, "but God's grace in me," enabling my will to do the good I do.

Reason 5. The judgment of the ancient church. Augustine [says]: "The will of the regenerate is kindled only by the Holy Ghost, that they may therefore be able because they will thus. And they will thus, because God works in them to will."[4] And,

4. In the margin: *August. de corrept. & grat. cap.* 12.

"we have lost our free will to love God by the greatness of our sin."[5] Sermon 2 on the words of the Apostle: "Man, when he was created, received a great strength in his free will, but by sinning he lost it." Fulgentius [says]: "God gives grace freely to the unworthy, whereby the wicked man, being justified, is enlightened *with the gift of goodwill* and with a *faculty of doing good.* That by mercy preventing him, he may *begin to will well*, and by mercy coming after he may do the good he will."[6] Bernard says, "It is wholly [by] the grace of God that we are created, healed, saved."[7] Council Arausic. 2, *cap.* 6: "To believe and to will is given from above by infusion and inspiration of the Holy Ghost." More testimonies and reasons might be alleged to prove this conclusion, but these shall suffice. Now let us see what reasons are alleged to the contrary.

III. Objections of Papists

Objection 1. First, they allege that man—by nature—may do that which is good, and therefore will that which is good; for none can do that which he neither wills nor thinks to do but first he must will and then do. Now, say they, men can do good by nature—as give alms, speak the truth, do justice, and practice other duties of civil virtue—and therefore will that which is good. *I answer*, that a natural man may do good works for the substance of the outward work, but not in regard of the goodness of the manner. These are two divers things. A man without supernatural grace may give alms, do justice, speak the truth, etc., which be good things considered in themselves as God has commanded them, but he cannot do them well. To think good things and to do good things are natural works. But to think good things in a good manner and to do them

5. In the margin: *Epist.* 105.

6. In the margin: *Fulg. lib. praed.*

7. In the margin: *Bernard li. de liber. arbitr.*

well, so as God may accept the action done, are works of grace. And therefore, the good thing done by a natural man is a sin in respect of the doer because it fails, both for his right beginning—which is a pure heart, good conscience, and faith unfeigned—as also for his end, which is the glory of God.

Objection 2. God has commanded all men to believe and repent. Therefore, they have natural free will by virtue whereof (being helped by the Spirit of God) they can believe and repent. *Answer.* This reason is not good, for by such commandments God shows not what men are able to do, but what they should do and what they cannot do. Again, the reason is not well framed; it ought rather to be thus: Because God gives men [the] commandment to repent and believe, therefore they have power to repent and believe, either by nature or by grace, and then we hold with them. For when God, in the gospel, commands men to repent and to believe, at the same time, by His grace, He enables them both to will or desire to believe and repent as also actually to repent and believe.

Objection 3. If man have no free will to sin or not to sin, then no man is to be punished for his sins—because he sins by a necessity not to be avoided. *Answer.* The reason is not good; for though man cannot but sin yet is the fault in himself and therefore he is to be punished. As a bankrupt is not therefore freed from his debts because he is not able to pay them, but the bills against him stand in force because the debt comes through his own default.

THE SECOND POINT

Of Original Sin

The next point to be handled is concerning original sin after baptism—that is, how far forth it remains after baptism. A point to be well considered, because hereupon depend many points of popery.

I. Our Consent

Conclusion 1. They say natural corruption after baptism is abolished, and so say we, but let us see how far it is abolished. In original sin are three things: 1. The punishment, which is the first and second death. 2. Guiltiness, which is the binding up of the creature unto punishment. 3. The fault or the offending of God, under which I comprehend our guiltiness in Adam's first offence as also the corruption of the heart, which is a natural inclination and proneness to anything that is evil or against the law of God. For the first, we say that after baptism in the regenerate, the punishment of original sin is taken away. "There is no condemnation (says the apostle) to them that be in Jesus Christ" (Rom. 8:1). For the second, that is the guiltiness, we further condescend and say that [it] is also taken away in them that are born anew. For considering there is no condemnation to them, there is nothing to bind them to punishment. Yet this caveat must be remembered, namely, that the guiltiness is removed from the person regenerate, not from the sin in the person. But of this, more afterward. Third, the guilt in Adam's first offence is pardoned. And touching the corruption of the heart, I avouch two things: 1. That the very power or strength whereby it reigns in man is taken away in the regenerate. 2. That this corruption is abolished (as also the fault of every actual sin past) so far forth as it is the fault and sin of the man in whom it is. Indeed, it remains until death, and it is sin considered in itself, so long as it remains, but it is not imputed unto the person. And in that respect it is as though it were not, it being pardoned.

II. The Dissent or Difference

Thus far we consent with the Church of Rome. Now the difference between us stands not in the abolishment, but in the manner and measure of the abolishment of this sin.

Papists teach that original sin is so far forth taken away after baptism that it ceases to be a sin properly, and is nothing else but a want, defect, and weakness, making the heart fit and ready to conceive sin. Much like tinder, which though it be no fire of itself, yet is it very apt and fit to conceive fire. And they, of the church of Rome, deny it to be sin properly, that they might uphold some gross opinions of theirs, namely, that a man in this life may fulfill the law of God, and do good works void of sin, [and] that he may stand righteous at the bar of God's judgment by them.

But we teach otherwise, that though original sin be taken away in the regenerate, and that in sundry respects, yet it remains in them after baptism, not only as a want and weakness, but as a sin—and that properly—as may by these reasons be proved:

Reason 1. Paul says directly, "It is no more I that do it, but sin that dwelleth in me" (Rom. 7:17), that is, original sin. The papists answer again that it is so-called improperly, because it comes of sin and also is an occasion of sin to be done. But by the circumstances of the text, it is sin properly; for in the words following, Saint Paul says that this sin dwelling in him made him to do the evil which he hated. And [in] v. 24, he cries out, "O wretched man that I am, who shall deliver me from this body of death!" Whence I reason thus:

> *That which once was sin properly, and still remaining in man makes him to sin, and entangles him in the punishment of sin, and makes him miserable, that is sin properly.*
> *But original sin doth all these. Ergo.*

Reason 2. Infants baptized and regenerate die the bodily death before they come to the years of discretion. Therefore, original sin in them is sin properly. Or else they should not die, having no cause of death in them, "For death is the wages of sin," as the Apostle says [in] Romans 6:23, and "Death entered into the world by sin" (Rom. 5:12). As for actual sin, they have none, if they die presently after they are born, before they come to any use either of reason or affection.

Reason 3. That which lusts against the Spirit, and by lusting tempts, and in tempting entices and draws the heart to sin, is for nature, sin itself. But concupiscence in the regenerate lists against the Spirit, Galatians 5:17, and tempts as I have said: "God tempteth no man, but every man is tempted when he is drawn away by his own concupiscence, and is enticed: then when lust conceiveth, it bringeth forth sin" (James 1:14). And therefore, it is sin properly; such as the fruit is, such is the tree. [According to] Augustine: "Concupiscence against which the spirit lusts, *is sin,* because in it there is disobedience against the rule of the mind; and it is the punishment of sin because it befalls man for the merits of his disobedience, and it is the cause of sin."[1]

Reason 4. The judgment of the ancient church. Augustine, [in] *Epist.* 29: "Charity in some is more, in some less, in some none. The highest degree of all which cannot be increased, is in none, as long as man lives upon earth. And as long as it may be increased, *that which is less than it should be is in fault*; by which fault it is, that there is no just man upon earth that does good and sins not; by which fault, none living shall be justified in the sight of God. For which fault, if we say we have no sin, there is no truth in us; for which also, though we profit never so much, it is necessary for us to say, 'Forgive us our debts,' though all our words, deeds, and thought be already forgiven in baptism." Indeed, Augustine in sundry places seems to deny concupiscence to be sin after baptism. But his meaning is that concupiscence in the regenerate is not the sin of the person in whom it is. For thus he expounds himself, "This is not to have sin, not to be guilty of sin."[2] And "The law of sin in baptism is remitted and not ended."[3] And "Let not sin reign. He says not, 'let not sin be,' but 'let it not reign.' For as long as you live, of necessity sin will be in your members. At the least, look it reign not in you."[4]

III. Objections of Papists

The arguments which the Church of Rome alleges to the contrary are these:

Objection 1. In baptism, men receive perfect and absolute pardon of sin; and sin being pardoned is taken quite away. And

1. In the margin: *Aug. contra Iul. l.* 5 *cap.* 3.
2. In the margin: *Ad Valer. lib.* 1 *cap.* 14.
3. In the margin: *Lib.* 2 *cont. Iul.*
4. In the margin: *Tract.* 42 *in Ioh.*

therefore, original sin after baptism ceases to be sin. *Answer.* Sin is abolished two ways: first, in regard of imputation to the person;[5] second, in regard of existing and being.[6] For this cause, God vouchsafes to man two blessings in baptism, *remission of sin* and *mortification* of the same. Remission, or pardon, abolishes sin wholly in respect of any imputation thereof unto man, but not simply in regard of the being thereof. Mortification therefore goes further and abolishes in all the powers of body and soul the very concupiscence or corruption itself, in respect of the being thereof. And because mortification is not accomplished until death, therefore original corruption remains until death, though not imputed.

Objection 2. Every sin is voluntary; but original sin in no man after baptism is voluntary, and therefore no sin. *Answer.* The proposition is a politic rule pertaining to the courts of men and must be understood of such actions as are done of one man to another. And it does not belong to the court of conscience, which God holds and keeps in men's hearts, in which every want of conformity to the law is made a sin. Second, I answer that original sin was voluntary in our first parent Adam; for he sinned and brought this misery upon us willingly, though in us it be otherwise upon just cause. Actual sin was first in him, and then original corruption. But in us original corruption is first, and then actual sin.

Objection 3. Where the form of any thing is taken away, there the thing itself ceases also. But after baptism in the regenerate, the form of original sin—that is, the guilt—is quite removed. And therefore, sin ceases to be sin. *Answer.* The guilt, or obligation to punishment, is not the form of original corruption, but (as we say in schools) an accident or necessary companion thereof. The true form of original sin is a defect and deprivation

5. In the margin: *Quoadimputationem.*

6. In the margin: *Quoadexistentiam.*

of that which the law requires at our hands in our mind, will, affections, and in all the powers both of soul and body. But they urge this reason further, saying, where the guilt and punishment is taken away, there is no fault remaining; but after baptism, the guilt and punishment are removed, and therefore, though original corruption remains, it is not as a fault to make us guilty before God, but only as a weakness. *Answer.* Guilt is removed, and not removed. It is removed from the person regenerate, which stands not guilty for any sin original or actual. But guilt is not removed from the sin itself. Or, as some answer, there be two kinds of guilt, actual and potential. The actual guilt is whereby sin makes man stand guilty before God, and that is removed in the regenerate; but the potential guilt—which is an aptness in sin to make a man stand guilty if he sin—that is not removed. And therefore, still sin remains sin. To this, or like effect, says Augustine: "We say that the guilt of concupiscence, not whereby *it is guilty* (for that is not a person) but that whereby it made man guilty from the beginning, is pardoned, and that the thing *itself is evil*, so as the regenerate desire to be healed of this plague."[7]

Objection 4. Lastly, for our disgrace, they allege that we—in our doctrine— teach that original sin, after baptism, is only clipped or pared, like the hair of a man's head, whose roots still remain in the flesh, growing and increasing after they are cut, as before. *Answer.* Our doctrine is abused. For in the paring of anything, as in cutting of the hair or in lopping a tree, the root remains untouched, and thereupon multiplies as before. But in the mortification of original sin after baptism, we hold no such paring, but teach that in the very first instant of the conversion of a sinner, sin receives his deadly wound in the root, never afterward to be recovered.

7. In the margin: *Contra Julian lib. 6. cap. 6.*

THE THIRD POINT

Certainty of Salvation

I. Our Consent

Conclusion 1. We hold and believe that a man – in this life – may be certain of salvation; and the same thing the Church of Rome teaches and holds.

Conclusion 2. We hold and believe that a man is to put a certain assurance in God's mercy in Christ for the salvation of his soul, and the same thing by common consent holds the foresaid church. This point makes not the difference between us.

Conclusion 3. We hold that, with assurance of salvation in our hearts, is joined doubting; and there is no man so assured of his salvation but he at some time doubts thereof, especially in the time of temptation. And in this the papists agree with us, and we with them.

Conclusion 4. They go further and say that a man may be certain of the salvation of men—or of the church—by catholic faith. And so say we.

Conclusion 5. Yes, they hold that a man by faith may be assured of his own salvation through extraordinary revelation, as Abraham and others were. And so do we.

Conclusion 6. They teach that we are to be certain of our salvation by special faith in regard of God that promises; though in regard of ourselves and our indisposition we cannot. And in the former point they consent with us.[1]

II. The Dissent or Difference

The very main point of difference lies in the manner of assurance.

Conclusion 1. We hold that a man may be certain of his salvation in his own conscience even in this life, and that by an ordinary and special faith. They hold that a man is certain of his salvation only by hope. Both of us hold a certainty; we by faith, they by hope.

Conclusion 2. Further, we hold and avouch that our certainty by true faith is infallible. They say their certainty is only probable.

Conclusion 3. And further, though both of us say that we have confidence in God's mercy in Christ for our salvation, yet we do it with some difference. For our confidence comes from certain and ordinary faith—theirs from hope, ministering (as they say) but a conjectural certainty.

Thus much of the difference. Now let us see the reason to and fro.

III. Objections of the Papists

Objection 1. Where there is no word, there is no faith, for these two are relatives. But there is no word of God saying, "Cornelius, believe," [or] "Peter, believe, and you shall be saved." And therefore, there is no such ordinary faith to believe a man's own particular salvation. *Answer.* The proposition is false, unless it be supplied with a clause on this manner: "Where there is no word of promise,

1. In the margin: *Bellar. l.* 3. *p.* 1129. *cl.*

nor anything that countervails a particular promise, there is no faith." "But," say they, "there is no such particular word. It is true, God does not speak to men particularly, 'Believe, and you shall be saved.' But yet He does that which is answerable hereunto, in that He gives a general promise, with a commandment to apply the same, and has ordained the holy ministry of the Word to apply the same to the person of the hearers in His own name. And that is as much as if the Lord himself should speak to men particularly." To speak more plainly, in the Scripture, the promises of salvation are indefinitely propounded. It says not anywhere, "If John will believe, he shall be saved," or, "If Peter will believe he shall be saved," but, "Whosoever believes shall be saved." Now then comes the minister of the Word, who standing in the room of God, and in the stead of Christ Himself, takes the indefinite promises of the gospel, and lays them to the hearts of every particular man. And this, in effect, is as much as if Christ Himself should say, "Cornelius believe, and you shall be saved." "Peter believe, and you shall be saved." It is answered that this applying of the gospel is upon condition of men's faith and repentance, and that men are deceived touching their own faith and repentance, and therefore fail in applying the Word unto themselves. *Answer.* Indeed, this manner of applying is false in all hypocrites, heretics, and unrepentant persons, for they apply upon carnal presumption, and not by faith. Nevertheless, it is true in all the elect, having the Spirit of grace and prayer; for when God, in the ministry of the Word, being His own ordinance, says, "Seek ye my face," the heart of God's children truly answers, "O Lord, I will seek thy face" (Ps. 27:8). And when God shall say, "Thou art my people," they shall say again, "The Lord is my God" (Zech. 13:9). And it is a truth of God that he which believes knows that he believes. And he that truly repents knows that he repents, unless it be in the beginning of our conversion, and in the time of distress and temptation. Otherwise, what thankfulness can there be for grace received?

Objection 2. It is no article of the creed that a man must believe his own salvation, and therefore no man is bound thereto. *Answer.* By this argument it appears plainly that the very pillars of the Church of Rome do not understand the creed, for in that which is commonly called the Apostles' Creed every article implies in it this particular faith. And in the first article, *I believe in God*, are three things contained: the first, to believe that there is a God; the second, to believe the same God is my God; the third, to put my confidence in Him for my salvation. And so much contain the other articles which are concerning God. When Thomas said, "My God" (John 20:28), Christ answered, "Thou hast believed, Thomas," where we see that to believe in God is to believe God to be our God. And Psalm 78:22, to believe in God and to put trust in Him are all one: "They believed not in God and trusted not in his help." And the articles concerning *remission of sins* and *life everlasting* do include, and we in them acknowledge our special faith concerning our own salvation. For to believe this or that is to believe there is such a thing and that the same thing belongs to me, as when David said, "I should have fainted except I had believed to see the goodness of the Lord in the land of the living" (Ps. 27:13). It is answered, that in those articles, we only profess ourselves to believe remission of sins, and life everlasting to be vouchsafed to the people and church of God. *Answer.* This indeed is the exposition of many, but it stands not with common reason. For if that be all the faith that is there confessed, the devil has as good a faith as we. He knows and believes that there is a God, and that this God imparts remission of sins and life everlasting to His church. And to the end that we, being God's children, may in faith go beyond all the devils in hell, we must further believe that remission of sins and life everlasting belong unto us. And unless we do particularly apply the said articles unto ourselves, we shall little or nothing differ from the devil in making confession of faith.

Objection 3. We are taught to pray for the pardon of our sins day by day (Matt. 6:12). And all this were needless if we could be assured of pardon in this life. *Answer.* The fourth petition must be understood not so much of our old debts or sins as of our present and new sins. For as we go on from day to day, so we add sin to sin; and for the pardon of them must we humble ourselves and pray.

I answer again that we pray for the pardon of our sins—not because we have no assurance thereof—but because [our] assurance is weak and small; we grow on from grace to grace in Christ as children do to man's estate by little and little. The heart of every believer is like a vessel with a narrow neck, which, being cast into the sea is not filled at the first; but by reason of the straight passage, receives water drop by drop. God gives unto us in Christ even a sea of mercy, but the same on our parts is apprehended and received only by little and little, as faith grows from age to age. And this is the cause why men having assurance pray for more.

Our Reasons to the Contrary

Reason 1. The first reason may be taken from the nature of faith on this manner. True faith is both an infallible assurance, and a particular assurance of the remission of sins, and of life everlasting. And therefore, by this faith, a man may be certainly and particularly assured of the remission of sins and life everlasting. That this reason may be of force, two things must be proved: First, that true faith is a certain assurance of God's mercy to that party in whom it is. Second, that faith is a particular assurance thereof. For the first, that faith is a certain assurance, Christ says to Peter, "O thou of little faith, wherefore didst thou doubt?" (Matt. 14:31)—Where he makes an opposition between faith and doubting—thereby giving us directly to understand that to be certain, and to give assurance, is of the nature of faith. Paul says of Abraham that he did not "doubt of the promise of God through unbelief, but was strengthened in the faith, and gave glory to God, being fully assured that He which had promised was able to do it" (Rom. 4:20–21). Where I observe first that doubting is made a fruit of unbelief; and therefore, infallible certainty and assurance, being contrary to doubting, must needs proceed from true faith—considering that contrary effects come of contrary causes, and contrary causes produce contrary effects. Second, I note that the strength of Abraham's faith did stand in "fullness of assurance," for the text says he was strengthened in the faith, being fully assured. And again, [in] Heb. 11:1, true saving faith is said to be the ground and substance of things hoped for, and the evidence or demonstration of things that are not seen. But faith can be no ground or evidence of things, unless it be for nature certainty itself. And thus, the first point is manifest. The second, that saving faith is a particular assurance, is proved by this, that the property of faith is to apprehend and apply the promise and the thing promised, Christ with His benefits. "As many," says Saint John, "as received him, to them he gave power to be the sons of God, namely, to them that believe in his name" (John 1:12). In these words, to believe in Christ, and to receive Christ, are put for one and the same thing. Now to receive Christ is to apprehend and apply Him with all His benefits unto ourselves as He is offered in the promises of the gospel. For in the sixth chapter following, first of all He sets forth Himself not only as a Redeemer generally, but also as the bread of life and the water of life. Second, He sets forth His best hearers as eaters of His body and drinkers of His blood. And third, He intends to prove this conclusion, that to eat His body and to drink His blood, and to believe in Him, are all one. Now then, if Christ be as food, and if to eat and drink the body and blood of Christ be to believe in Him, then must there be a proportion between eating and believing. Look then, as there can be no eating without taking or receiving of meat, so no believing in Christ without a spiritual receiving and apprehending of Him. And as the body has his hand, mouth, and stomach, whereby it takes, receives, and digests meat for the nourishment of every part, so likewise, in the soul there is a faith which is both hand, mouth, and stomach to apprehend, receive, and apply Christ and all His merits for the nourishment of the soul. And Paul says yet more plainly, that "through faith we receive the promise of the Spirit" (Gal. 3:14).

Now as the property of apprehending and applying of Christ belongs to faith, so it agrees not to hope, love, confidence, or any other gift or grace of God. But first, by faith we must apprehend Christ, and apply Him to ourselves, before we can have any hope or confidence in Him. And this applying seems not to be done by any affection of the will, but by a supernatural act of the mind, which is to acknowledge, set down, and believe that remission of sins, and life everlasting by the merit of Christ, belong to us particularly. To this which I have said agrees Augustine, [in] *Tract.* 25, on John: "Why prepare your teeth and belly? Believe, and you have eaten." And, [in] *Tract.* 50: "How shall I reach my hand into heaven, that I may hold Him sitting there? Send up your faith, and you lay hold on Him." And Bernard says, *homil. in Cat.* 76, "Where He is, you cannot come now...yet go to, follow Him, and seek Him...believe, and you have found Him. For to believe is to find." Chrysostom on Mark., *Homil.* 10: "Let us believe and we see Jesus present before us." Ambrose on Luke *lib.* 6. *c.* 8: "By faith Christ is touched, by faith Christ is seen." Tertul. *de resur., car.*: "He must be chewed by understanding and be digested by faith."

Reason 2. Whatsoever the Holy Ghost testifies unto us, that we may, yes, that we must certainly by faith believe. But the Holy Ghost particularly testifies unto us our adoption, the remission of our sins, and the salvation of our souls. And therefore, we may and must particularly and certainly by faith believe the same. The first part of this reason is true, and cannot be denied of any. The second part is proved thus: Saint Paul says [in] Romans 8:15, "We have not received the spirit of bondage to fear; but the spirit of adoption, whereby we cry Abba, Father," adding further that "the same Spirit bears witness with our spirits, that we are the children of God." Where the apostle makes two witnesses of our adoption: the Spirit of God, and our spirits, that is, the conscience sanctified by the Holy Ghost. The papists, to elude this reason, allege that the Spirit of God indeed witnesses of our adoption by some comfortable feeling of God's love and favor, being such as [it] is weak and oftentimes deceitful. But by their leave, the testimony of the Spirit is more than a bare sense or feeling of God's grace. For it is called the *pledge* and *earnest* of God's Spirit in our hearts [2 Cor. 1:22], and therefore it is fit to take away all occasion of doubting of our salvation, as in a bargain the earnest is given between the parties to put all out of question. Bernard says that the testimony of the Spirit is a most sure testimony, *Epist.* 107.

Reason 3. That which we must pray for by God's commandment, that we must believe. But every man is to pray for the pardon of his own sins and for life everlasting. Of this there is no question—therefore he is bound to believe the same. The proposition is most of all doubtful, but it is proved thus. In every petition there must be two things: a desire of the things we ask, and a particular faith whereby we believe that the thing we ask shall be given unto us. So Christ says, "Whatsoever ye desire when you pray, believe that you shall have it, and it shall be given unto you" (Mark 11:24). And Saint John further notes out this particular faith, calling it our "assurance, that God will give unto us whatsoever we ask according to his will" (1 John 5:14). And hence it is, that in every petition there must be two grounds: a commandment to warrant us in making a petition, and a promise to assure us of the accomplishment thereof. And upon both these follows necessarily an application of the things we ask to ourselves.

Reason 4. Whatsoever God commands in the gospel, that a man must and can perform; but God in the gospel commands us to believe the pardon of our own sins, and life everlasting, and therefore we must believe thus much and may be assured thereof. This proposition is plain by the distinction of the commandments, of the law, and of the gospel. The commandments of the law show us what we must do but minister no power to perform the thing to be done. But the doctrine and commandment of the gospel do otherwise; and therefore, they are called *spirit* and *life* [John 6:63], God with the commandment giving grace that the thing prescribed may be done. Now this is a commandment of the gospel, to believe remission of sins, for it was the substance of Christ's ministry, "Repent and believe the gospel". And that is not generally to believe that Christ is a Savior, and that the promises made in Him are true (for so the devils believe with trembling), but it is particularly to believe that Christ is my Savior, and that the promises of salvation in Christ belong especially to me, as Saint John says, "This is his commandment, that we believe in the name of Jesus Christ" (1 John 3:23). Now to believe in Christ is to put confidence in Him, which none can do, unless he be first assured of His love and favor. And therefore, in as much as we are enjoined to put our confidence in Christ, we are also enjoined to believe our reconciliation with him, which stands in the remission of our sins, and our acceptation to life everlasting.

Reason 5. Whereas the papists teach that a man may be assured of his salvation by hope, even hence it follows that he may be infallibly assured thereof. For the property of true and lively hope "is never to make a man ashamed" (Rom. 5:5). And true hope follows faith and presupposes certainty of faith. Neither can any man truly hope for his salvation unless by faith he be certainly assured thereof in some measure.

The popish doctors make exception to these reasons on this manner.[2]

Exception 1. First, they say it cannot be proved that a man is as certain of his salvation by faith as he is of the articles of the creed. *Answer.* First, they prove thus much, that we ought to be as certain of the one as of the other. For look, what commandment we have to believe the articles of our faith, the like we have enjoining us to believe the pardon of our own sins, as I have proved. Second, these arguments prove it to be the nature or essential property of faith, as certainly to assure man of his salvation as it assures him of the articles which he believes. And howsoever commonly men do not believe their salvation as infallible, as they do their articles of faith, yet some special men do, having God's word applied by the Spirit as a sure ground of their faith, whereby they believe their own salvation, as they have it for a ground of the articles of their faith. Thus certainly was Abraham assured of his own salvation, as also the prophets and apostles, and the martyrs of God in all ages; whereupon without doubting they have been content to lay down their lives for the name of Christ, in whom they are assured to receive eternal happiness. And there is no question, but there be many now, that by long and often experience of God's mercy, and by the inward certificate of the Holy Ghost, have attained to a full assurance of their salvation.

---

2. This paragraph break is not in the original.

Exception 2. Howsoever a man may be assured of his present estate, yet no man is certain of his perseverance unto the end. *Answer.* It is otherwise. For in the sixth petition, "lead us not into temptation," we pray that God would not suffer us to be wholly overcome of the devil in any temptation; and to this petition we have a promise answerable, "That God with the temptation will give an issue" (1 Cor. 10:13), and therefore howsoever the devil may buffet, molest, and wound the servants of God, yet shall he never be able to overcome them. Again, he that is once a member of Christ can never be wholly cut off. And if any by sin were wholly severed from Christ for a time, in his recovery he is to be baptized the second time, for baptism is the sacrament of initiation or engrafting into Christ. By this reason we should as often be baptized as we fall into any sin, which is absurd. Again Saint John says, "They went out from us, but they were not of us: for if they had been of us, they would have continued with us" (1 John 2:19).[3] Where he takes it for granted that such as be once in Christ shall never wholly be severed or fall from Him. Though our communion with Christ may be lessened, yet the union and the bond of conjunction is never dissolved. *Exception 3.* They say, we are indeed to believe our salvation on God's part, but we must needs doubt in regard of ourselves, because the promises of remission of sins are given upon condition of man's faith and repentance. Now we cannot (say they) be assured that we have true faith and repentance, because we may lie in secret sins, and so want that indeed, which we suppose ourselves to have. *Answer.* I say again, he that truly repents and believes, by God's grace knows that he repents and believes; or else Paul would never have said, "Prove yourselves whether you be in the faith or not" (2 Cor. 13:5). And the same apostle says, "We have not received

3. The 1635 edition incorrectly indicates 1 John 1:19.

the spirit of the world, but the spirit which is of God, that we might *know* the things which are given of God" (1 Cor. 2:12), which things are not only life everlasting, but justification, sanctification, and such like. And as for secret sins, they cannot make our repentance void. For he that truly repents of his known sins repents also of such as be unknown and receives the pardon of them all. God requires not an express or special repentance of unknown sins, but accepts it as sufficient, if we repent of them generally. As David says, "Who knows the errors of this life? Forgive me my secret sins" (Ps. 19:12). And whereas they add that faith and repentance must be sufficient, I answer that the sufficiency of our faith and repentance stands in the truth, and not in the measure or perfection thereof; and the truth of both, where they are, is certainly discerned.

Reason 6. The judgment of the ancient church. Augustine: "Of an evil servant you are made a good [servant]. Therefore, *presume* not of your own doing, but of the grace of Christ; it is not arrogance, *but faith*. To acknowledge what you have received, it is not pride, but devotion."[4] And, "Let no man ask another man, but return to his own heart. If he finds charity there, he *has security* for his passage from life to death."[5] Hilary on Matthew 5: "The kingdom of heaven, which our Lord professed to be in himself, his will is that it must be hoped for *without any doubtfulness of uncertain will*. Otherwise there is no justification by faith, if faith itself be made doubtful." Bernard, in his epist. 107: "Who is the just man, but he that being loved of God, loves Him again; which comes not to pass but by the *Spirit revealing by faith* the eternal *purpose of God* of His *salvation* to come. Which revelation is nothing else but infusion of spiritual grace, by which,

4. In the margin: *De verbis Dei serm.* 28.

5. In the margin: *Tract.* 5 *in epist. Joh.*

when the deeds of the flesh are mortified, the man is prepared to the kingdom of heaven.... Together receiving in one Spirit that whereby he *may presume* that he is loved and also love again..."

To conclude, the papists have no great cause to dissent from us in this point. For they teach and profess that they do by a special faith believe their own salvation certainly and infallibly in respect of God that promises. Now the thing which hinders them is their own indisposition and unworthiness (as they say) which keeps them from being certain otherwise than in a likely hope. But this hindrance is easily removed, if men will judge indifferently. For first of all, in regard of ourselves and our disposition, we cannot be certain at all, but must despair of salvation even to the very death. We cannot be sufficiently disposed so long as we live in this world, but must always say with Jacob, "I am less than all thy mercies" (Gen. 32:10), and with David, "Enter not into judgment with thy servant, O Lord, for none living shall be justified in thy sight" (Ps. 143:2),[6] and with the centurion, "Lord I am not worthy, that thou shouldest come under my roof" (Matt. 8:8). Second, God, in making promise of salvation, respects not men's worthiness. For He chose us to life everlasting when we were not; He redeemed us from death being enemies and entitles us to the promise of salvation "if we acknowledge ourselves to be sinners" (Matt. 9:13). "If we labor and travail under the burden of them" (Matt. 11:28). "If we hunger and thirst after grace" (John 7:37). And these things we may certainly and sensibly perceive in ourselves, and when we find them in us, though our unworthiness be exceeding great, it should not hinder our assurance. For God makes manifest His power in our weakness (2 Cor. 12:9), and He will not break the bruised reed nor quench the smoking flax (Isa. 42:3). Third, if a man love God for His mercies' sake, and have a

6. In the 1635 edition, the note in margin incorrectly indicates Ps. 143:10 instead of Ps. 143:2.

true hope of salvation by Christ, he is in Christ and has fellowship with Him. And he that is in Christ has all his unworthiness and wants laid on Christ, and they are covered and pardoned in His death. And in respect of ourselves thus considered *as we are in Christ*, we have no cause to waver, but to be certain of our salvation, and that in regard of ourselves.

THE FOURTH POINT

Touching the Justification of a Sinner

That we may see how far we are to agree with them and where to differ, first I will set down the doctrine on both parts, and second the main difference wherein we are to stand against them, even to death.

Our doctrine touching the justification of a sinner, I propound in four rules:

Rule 1. That justification is an action of God, whereby He absolves a sinner and accepts him to life everlasting for the righteousness and merit of Christ.

Rule 2. That justification stands in two things: first, in the remission of sins by the merit of Christ's death; second, in the imputation of Christ's own righteousness, which is another action of God whereby He accounts and esteems that righteousness which is in Christ, as the righteousness of that sinner which believes in Him. By Christ's own righteousness we are to understand two things: first, His sufferings, especially in His death and passion. Second, His obedience in fulfilling the law—both which go together, for Christ in suffering obeyed, and obeying suffered. And the very shedding of His blood to which our salvation is ascribed must not only be considered as it is passive, that is, a suffering, but also as it is active, that is, an obedience, in which He showed His exceeding love both to His Father and us, and thus fulfilled the law for us. This point, if some had well thought on, they would not have placed all [of] justification in remission of sins as they do.

Rule 3. That justification is from God's mere mercy and grace, procured only by the merit of Christ.

Rule 4. That man is justified by faith alone; because faith is that alone instrument created in the heart by the Holy Ghost, whereby a sinner lays hold of Christ's own righteousness, and applies the same unto himself. There is neither hope, nor love, nor any other grace of God within man that can do this but faith alone.

The doctrine of the Roman Church touching the justification of a sinner is on this manner:

They hold that before justification there goes a preparation thereunto; which is an action wrought partly by the Holy Ghost, and partly by the power of natural free will, whereby a man disposes himself to his own future justification.

In the preparation they consider the ground of justification, and things proceeding from it. The ground is faith, which they define to be a general knowledge, whereby we understand and believe that the doctrine of the Word of God is true. Things proceeding from this faith are these: a sight of our sins, a fear of hell, hope of salvation, love of God, repentance, and such like—all which, when men have attained, they are then fully disposed (as they say) to their justification.

This preparation being made, then comes justification itself, which is an action of God whereby He makes a man righteous. It has two parts: the first and the second. The first is when a sinner of an evil man is made a good man. And to effect this, two things are required: first, the pardon of sin, which is one part of the first justification; second, the infusion of inward righteousness, whereby the heart is purged and sanctified, and this habit of righteousness stands especially in hope and charity.

After the first justification follows the second, which is, when a man of a good or just man is made better and more just. And this, say they, may proceed from works of grace, because he which is righteous by the first justification can bring forth good works, by the merit whereof he is able to make himself more just and righteous. And yet they grant that the first justification comes only of God's mercy by the merit of Christ.

I. Our Consent[1] and Difference

Now let us come to the points of difference between us and them touching justification.

The first main difference is in the matter thereof, which shall be seen by the answer both of Protestant and papist to this one question, "What is the very thing that causes a man to stand righteous before God and to be accepted to life everlasting?" We answer: Nothing but the righteousness of Christ, which consists partly in His sufferings, and partly in His active obedience in fulfilling the rigor of the law. And here let us consider how near the papists come to this answer, and wherein they dissent.

Consent 1. They grant that in justification, sin is pardoned by the merits of Christ, and that none can be justified without remission of sins. And that is well.

Consent 2. They grant that the righteousness whereby a man is made righteous before God comes from Christ, and from Christ alone.

1. The 1635 edition incorrectly has "Dissent" instead of "Consent."

Consent 3. The most learned among them say that Christ's satisfaction and the merit of His death, is imputed to every sinner that believes for His satisfaction before God.[2] And hitherto we agree.

The very point of difference is this: we hold that the satisfaction made by Christ in His death and obedience to the law is imputed to us and becomes our righteousness. They say it is our satisfaction and not our righteousness whereby we stand righteous before God, because it is inherent in the person of Christ as in a subject. Now the answer of the papist to the former question is on this manner: The thing (says he) that makes us righteous before God and causes us to be accepted to life everlasting is remission of sins, and the habit of inward righteousness, or charity with the fruits thereof. We condescend and grant that the habit of righteousness, which we call sanctification, is an excellent gift of God, and has its reward of God, and is the matter of our justification before man, because it serves to declare us to be reconciled to God, and to be justified. Yet we deny it to be the thing which makes us of sinners to become righteous or just before God.

And this is the first point of our disagreement in the matter of justification, which must be marked, because if there were no more points of difference between us, this one alone were sufficient to keep us from [the] uniting of our religions. For hereby the Church of Rome razes the very foundation.

Now let us see by what reasons we justify our doctrine, and second, answer the contrary objections.

Our Reasons

Reason 1. That very thing which must be our righteousness before God must satisfy the justice of the law, which says, "do these things and thou shalt live" [Rom. 10:5]. Now there is nothing can satisfy the justice of the law but the righteousness

2. In the margin: *Bellar. de Iustif. l. 2 cap. 7.*

or obedience of Christ for us. If any allege civil justice, it is nothing, for Christ says, "Except your righteousness exceed the righteousness of the scribes and Pharisees, ye cannot enter into the kingdom of heaven" [Matt. 5:20]. What? Shall we say that works make us just? That cannot be, for all men's works are defective in respect of the justice of the law. Shall we say our sanctification, whereby we are renewed to the image of God in righteousness and true holiness? That also is imperfect and cannot satisfy God's justice required in the law, as Isaiah has said of himself and the people, "all our righteousness is as a menstruous cloth" (Isa. 64:6).[3] To have a clear conscience before God is a principal part of inward righteousness; and of it Paul in his own person says thus, "I am privy to nothing by myself, yet am I not justified thereby" (1 Cor. 4:4). Therefore, nothing can procure unto us an absolution and acceptance to life everlasting but Christ's imputed righteousness. And this will appear if we do consider how we must come one day before God's judgment seat, there to be judged in the rigor of justice. For then we must bring something that may countervail the justice of God, not having only acceptation in mercy, but also approbation in justice, God being not only merciful, but also a just judge.

Reason 2. "He which knew no sin, was made sin for us, that we might be made the righteousness of God which is in him" (2 Cor. 5:21). Whence I reason thus: As Christ was made sin for us, so are we made the righteousness of God in Him. But Christ was made sin, or, a sinner by imputation of our sins, He being in Himself most holy; therefore a sinner is made righteous before God in that Christ's righteousness is imputed and applied unto him. Now if any shall say that man is justified by righteousness infused, then by like reason I say Christ was made sin for us by

3. The 1635 edition incorrectly cites *Isa. 46:6* in the margin.

infusion of sin, which to say is blasphemy. And the exposition of this place by Saint Jerome is not to be despised. "Christ," says he, "being offered for our sins, took the name of sin, that we might be made the righteousness of God in Him, not ours nor in us." If this righteousness of God be neither ours nor in us, then it can be no inherent righteousness, but must needs be righteousness imputed. And Chrysostom on this place says, "It is called God's righteousness, because it is not of works, and because it must be *without all stain* or want," and this cannot be inherent righteousness. Anselm says, "He is made sin as we are made justice; not ours but God's. Not in us but in Him—as He is made sin, not His own, but ours—not in Himself, but in us."

Reason 3. "As by one man's disobedience many were made sinners: so by the obedience of one shall many be made righteous" (Rom. 5:19). Mark, here is a comparison between the first and second Adam. And hence I reason thus: as by the disobedience of the first Adam, men were made sinners, so by the obedience of the second Adam are we made righteous. Now we are not only made sinners by propagation of natural corruption, but by imputation. For Adam's first sin was the eating of the forbidden fruit, which very act is no personal offence, but is imputed to all his posterity, "in whom we have all sinned." The Fathers call this very sin Adam's handwriting, making us debtors unto God.[4] And therefore, in like manner, the obedience of Christ is made the righteousness of every believer, not by infusion but by imputation.

Reason 4. A satisfaction made for the want of that justice or obedience which the law requires at our hands is accepted of God as the justice itself. But Christ's obedience is a satisfaction made for the want of that justice or obedience which the law requires,

4. In the margin: *Iren. lib.* 5. *cap.* 17. *Chrysostom. homil. ad Neoph.*

as the papists themselves avouch. Therefore, this satisfaction is our justice. And methinks, the papists upon this consideration have little cause to dissent from us. For if they make Christ's obedience their salvation, why should they not fully close hands with us and make it their justice also?

Reason 5. The consent of the ancient church. Bernard says, *epist.* 190: "*The justice of another* is assigned unto man, who wanted his own. Man was indebted, and man made payment. The *satisfaction* of one is imputed to all. And, why may not justice be from another, as well as guiltiness is from another?" And in Cant. *serm.* 25: "It suffices me for all righteousness, to have Him alone merciful to me, against whom I have sinned." And, "Not to sin is God's justice, *man's justice* is the *mercifulness of God.*" And *serm.* 61: "Shall I sing my own righteousness? Lord, I will remember your righteousness alone, for *it is mine also*, in that even you are made unto me [the] righteousness of God. What, shall I fear lest that one be not sufficient for us both? It is not a short cloak that cannot cover two; it will cover both you and me largely, being both a large and eternal justice." Augustine on Psalm 22: "He prays for our faults and has made our faults His faults, that He might make *His justice our justice.*"

Objections of Papists

[The] objections of the papists proving inherent righteousness to be in the matter of our injustice before God are these:[5]

Objection 1. It is absurd that one man should be made righteous by the righteousness of another, for it is as much as if one man were made wise by the wisdom of another. *Answer.* It is true that no man can be made righteous by the personal righteousness of another—because it pertains only to one man. And because the wisdom that is in one man, is his altogether wholly,

5. This paragraph break is not in the original.

it cannot be the wisdom of another, no more than the health and life of one body, can be the health of another. But it is otherwise with the righteousness of Christ. It is His indeed, because it is inherent in Him as a subject. It is not His alone but His and ours together by the tenor of the covenant of grace. Christ, as He is a Mediator, is given to every believer as really and truly, as land is given from man to man, and with Him are given all things that concern salvation, they being made ours by God's free gift, among which is Christ His righteousness. By it therefore, as being a thing of our own, we may be justified before God, and accepted to life everlasting.

Objection 2. If a sinner be justified by Christ His righteousness, then every believer shall be as righteous as Christ, and that cannot be. *Answer.* The proposition is false. For Christ His righteousness is not applied to us according as it is in Christ, neither according to the same measure, nor the same manner. For His obedience in fulfilling the law is above Adam's righteousness, yes above the righteousness of all angels. For they were all but creatures, and their obedience the obedience of creatures, but Christ's obedience is the obedience or righteousness of God—so termed, [Rom. 1:17, 18; 2 Cor. 5:21], not only because God accepted of it, but because it was in that person which is very God. When Christ obeyed, God obeyed. And when He suffered, God suffered—not because the Godhead suffered or performed any obedience, but because the person which [was] according to one nature in God, performed obedience and suffered. And by this means His righteousness is of infinite value, price, merit, and efficacy. Hence also it comes to pass that this obedience of Christ serves not only for the justifying of some one person (as Adam's did[6]) but of all and every one of the elect. Yes, it is sufficient to justify many

6. In the margin: Namely, for himself.

thousand worlds. Now to come to the point, this righteousness that is in Christ, in this largeness and measure, is pertaining to us in a more narrow scantling;[7] because it is only received by faith so far forth as it serves to justify any particular believer.[8] But they urge the reason further, saying, "If Christ His righteousness be the righteousness of every believer, then every man should be a Savior, which is absurd." *Answer.* I answer as before and yet more plainly thus: Christ His righteousness is imputed to the person of this or that man, not as it is the price of redemption for all mankind, but as it is the price of redemption for one particular man. As for example, Christ's righteousness is imputed to Peter, not as it is the price of redemption for all, but as it is the price of redemption for Peter. And therefore, Christ's righteousness is not applied to any one sinner in that largeness and measure in which it is in the Person of Christ, but only so far forth as it serves to satisfy the law for the said sinner, and to make his person accepted of God as righteous, and no further.

Objection 3. If we be made righteous by Christ's righteousness truly, then Christ is a sinner truly by our sins. But Christ is not indeed a sinner by our sins. *Answer.* We may with reverence to His majesty, in good manner say that Christ was a sinner, and that truly, not by any infusion of sin into His most holy person, but because our sins were laid on Him. Thus, says the Holy Ghost, "He which knew no sin was made sin for us" (2 Cor. 5:21), and He was counted with sinners (Isa. 53:12), yet so as even then, in Himself He was without blot, yes more holy than all men and angels. On this manner said Chrysostom, [on] 2 Corinthians 5, "God permitted Christ to be condemned as a

---

7. *Scantling:* a small amount of something.

8. In the margin: As any one star partakes in the whole light of the sun with the rest of the stars, so far forth as the said light makes it to shine.

sinner." Again, "He made the just one to be a *sinner*, that He might make sinners just."

Objection 4. If a man be made righteous by imputation, then God judges sinners to be righteous. But God judges no sinner to be righteous, for it is abomination to the Lord. *Answer.* When God justifies a sinner by Christ's righteousness, at the same time he ceases in regard of guiltiness to be a sinner. And to whom God imputes righteousness, them He sanctifies at the very same instant by His Holy Spirit, giving also unto original corruption His deadly wound.

Objection 5. That which Adam never lost was never given by Christ. But he never lost imputed righteousness; therefore, it was never given unto him. *Answer.* The proposition is not true, for saving faith—that was never lost by Adam—is given to us in Christ. And Adam never had this privilege, that after the first grace should follow the second.[9] And thereupon, being left to himself, he fell from God. And yet this mercy is vouchsafed to all believers that after their first conversion, God will still confirm them with new grace. And by this means they persevere unto the end. And whereas they say that Adam had not imputed righteousness, I answer that he had the same for substance, though not for the manner of applying by imputation.

Objection 6. Justification is eternal, but the imputation of Christ's righteousness is not eternal, for it ceases in the end of this life; therefore, it is not that which justifies a sinner. *Answer.* The imputation of Christ's righteousness is everlasting. For he that is esteemed righteous in this life by Christ's righteousness, is accepted as righteous forever; and the remission of sins granted in this life is forever continued. And though sanctification be perfect in the world to come, yet shall it not justify.

---

9. In the margin: We have *et posse et velle*; he had no more but *posse si vellet*, and he wanted *velle quod posset. Aug. de corrept. et grat. cap.* 11.

For we must conceive it no otherwise after this life, but as a fruit springing from the imputed righteousness of Christ, without which it could not be. And a good child will not cast away the first garment because his father gives him a second. And what if inward righteousness be perfect in the end of this life, shall we therefore make it the matter of our justification? God forbid, for the righteousness whereby sinners are justified must be had in the time of this life, before the pangs of death.

II. Difference about the Manner of Justification

All, both papists and Protestants, agree that a sinner is justified by faith. This agreement is only in word, and the difference between us is great indeed. And it may be reduced to these three heads:[10]

First, the papist saying, that a man is justified by faith, understands a general or a catholic faith, whereby a man believes the articles of religion to be true. But we hold that the faith which justifies is a particular faith, whereby we apply to ourselves the promises of righteousness and life everlasting by Christ. And that our opinion is the truth I have proved before, but [I] will add a reason or two.

Reason 1. The faith whereby we live is that faith whereby we are justified. But the faith whereby we live spiritually is a particular faith whereby we apply Christ unto ourselves, as Paul says, "I live," that is spiritually, "by the faith of the Son of God," which faith he shows to be a particular faith in Christ, in the very words following, "who has loved me and given himself *for me particularly*" (Gal. 2:20). And in this manner of believing Paul was and is an example to all that are to be saved [1 Tim 1:16 and Phil. 3:15, 17].

Reason 2. That which we are to ask of God in prayer we must believe it shall be given us, as we ask it. But in prayer we are to ask the pardon of our own sins, and the merit of Christ's righteousness

10. This paragraph break is not in the original.

for ourselves; therefore, we must believe the same particularly. The proposition is a rule of God's Word, requiring that, in every petition, we bring a particular faith whereby we believe that the thing lawfully asked shall be given accordingly [Mark 11:24]. The *minor* is also evident, neither can it be denied; for we are taught by Christ Himself to pray on this manner, "Forgive us our debts," and to it we say, "Amen," that is, that our petitions shall without doubt be granted unto us. [See] Augustine, *serm. de Temp.*, 182.

And here note that the Church of Rome in the doctrine of justification by faith cuts off the principal part and property thereof. For in justifying faith, two things are required: first, knowledge revealed in the Word touching the means of salvation; second, an applying of things known unto ourselves which some call affiance.[11] Now the first they acknowledge, but the second, which is the very substance and principal part thereof, they deny.

Reason 3. The judgment of the ancient church. Augustine: "I demand now, do you believe in Christ, O sinner? You say, I believe. What do you believe? That all your sins may freely be pardoned in Him. *You have that which you have believed.*"[12] Bernard: "The apostle thinks that a man is justified freely by faith. If you believe that your sins cannot be remitted, but by Him alone against whom they were committed, but go further and believe this too, that by him *your sins are forgiven you.* This is the testimony which the Holy Ghost gives in the heart, saying, 'Your sins are forgiven you.'"[13] Cyprian: "God promises you immortality when you go out of the world, and do *you doubt?* This is indeed not to know God, and this is for a member of the church in the house of faith not to have faith. If we believe in Christ, let us

11. *Affiance:* trust.

12. In the margin: *De verb. Dei, serm.* 7.

13. In the margin: *Serm. de Anun.*

believe His words and promises, and we shall never die, and shall come to Christ with *joyful security* with Him to reign forever."[14]

The second difference touching faith in the act of justification is this. The papist says we are justified by faith because it disposes a sinner to his justification after this manner: "By faith," says he, "the mind of man is enlightened in the knowledge of the law and gospel; knowledge stirs up a fear of hell with a consideration of the promise of happiness, as also the love and fear of God, and hope of life eternal. Now when the heart is thus prepared, God infuses the habit of charity and other virtues, whereby a sinner is justified before God." We say otherwise that faith justifies because it is a supernatural instrument created by God in the heart of man at his conversion, whereby he apprehends and receives Christ's righteousness for his justification.

In this their doctrine is a twofold error: 1. That they make faith which justifies, to go before justification itself, both for order of nature, as also for time; whereas by the Word of God, at the very instant when any man believes, first, he is then justified and sanctified, for he that believes, eats and drinks the body and blood of Christ, and is already passed from death to life [John 6:54].

The second is that faith being nothing else with them but an illumination of the mind, stirs up the will, which, being moved and helped, causes in the heart many spiritual motions, and thereby disposes man to his future justification. But this indeed is as much as if he should say, that dead men only helped, can prepare themselves to their future resurrection. For we are all by nature dead in sin, and therefore must not only be enlightened in mind, but also renewed in will, before we can so much as will or desire that which is good. Now we (as I have said) teach otherwise—that faith justifies as it is an instrument to apprehend and

14. In the margin: *Serm. de Natal.*

apply Christ with His obedience, which is the matter of our justification. This is the truth; I prove it thus: In the covenant of grace two things must be considered: the substance thereof and the condition. The substance of the covenant is that *righteousness and life everlasting is given to God's church and people by Christ.* The condition is that we for our parts are by faith to receive the foresaid benefits; and this condition is by grace as well as the substance. Now then, that we may attain to salvation by Christ, He must be given unto us really, as He is propounded in the tenor of the foresaid covenant. And for the giving of Christ, God has appointed special ordinances, as the preaching of the Word and the administration of the sacraments. The Word preached is the power of God to salvation to everyone that believes; and the end of the sacraments is to communicate Christ with all His benefits to them that come to be partakers thereof—as is most plainly to be seen in the Supper of the Lord, in which the giving of bread and wine to the several communicants is a pledge and sign of God's particular giving of Christ's body and blood with all His merits unto them. And this giving on God's part cannot be effectual without receiving on our parts; and therefore, faith must needs be an instrument or hand to receive that which God gives, that we may find comfort by His giving.

The third difference concerning faith is this: The papist says that a man is justified by faith, yet not by faith alone, but also by other virtues, as hope, love, the fear of God, etc. The reasons which are brought to maintain their opinion are of no moment:

Reason 1. "Many sins are forgiven her, *because* she loved much" (Luke 7:47). Whence they gather that the woman here spoken of was justified and had the pardon of her sins by love.[15] *Answer.* In this text, love is not made an impulsive

---

15. In the margin: *Particula non causalis, sed illatiua vel rationalis.*

cause to move God to pardon her sins, but only a sign to show and manifest that God had already pardoned them. Like to this is the place of John, who says, "We are translated from death to life, *because* we love the brethren" (1 John 3:14), where love is no cause of the change, but a sign and consequence thereof. *Reason 2.* "Neither circumcision, nor uncircumcision availeth anything, but faith that worketh by love" (Gal. 5:6). Hence, they gather that faith functions together with love. *Answer.* The property of true faith is to apprehend and receive something unto itself. And love, that goes always with faith—as a fruit and an inseparable companion thereof—is of another nature. For it does not receive in, but as it were, give[s] out itself in all the duties of the first and second table towards God and man. And this thing faith by itself cannot do, and therefore Paul says that faith works by love. The hand has a property to reach out itself, to lay hold of anything, and to receive a gift. But the hand has no property to cut a piece of wood of itself—without saw or knife or some like instrument—and yet by help of them it can either divide or cut. Even so, it is the nature of faith to go out of itself and to receive Christ into the heart. As for the duties of the first and second table, faith cannot of itself bring them forth; no more than the hand can divide or cut. Yet join love to faith and then can it practice duties commanded concerning God and man. And this I take to be the meaning of this text, which speaks not of justification by faith, but only of the practice of common duties, which faith puts in execution by the help of love.

Reason 3. Faith is never alone, therefore it does not justify alone. *Answer.* The reason is naught and they might as well dispute thus: The eye is never alone from the head, and therefore it sees not alone; which is absurd. And though in regard of substance the eye be never alone, yet in regard of seeing it is alone. And so, though faith subsist not without love and hope and other graces of God, yet in regard of the act of justification it is alone without them all.

Reason 4. If faith alone justifies, then we are saved by faith alone. But we are not saved by faith alone, and therefore [we are] not justified by faith alone. *Answer.* The proposition is false, for more things are requisite to the main end than to the subordinate means. And the assumption is false, for we are saved by faith alone if we speak of faith as it is an instrument apprehending Christ for our salvation.

Reason 5. "We are saved by hope," (Rom. 8:24), therefore not by faith alone. *Answer.* We are saved by hope, not because it is any cause of our salvation. Paul's meaning is only this: that we have not salvation as yet in possession but wait patiently for it—in time to come to be possessed of us—expecting the time of our full deliverance. That is all that can justly be gathered hence.

Now the doctrine which we teach on the contrary is, that a sinner is justified before God by faith, yea, by faith alone. The meaning is, that nothing within man and nothing that man can do—either by nature or by grace—concurs to the act of justification before God, as any cause thereof—either efficient, material, formal, or final—but faith alone. All other gifts and graces—as hope, love, the fear of God—are necessary to salvation, as signs thereof and consequents of faith. Nothing in any man concurs as any cause to this work but faith alone. And faith itself is no principal but only an instrumental cause whereby we receive, apprehend, and apply Christ and His righteousness for our justification.

Reason 1. "As Moses lifted up the serpent in the wilderness, so must the Son of Man be lifted up: that whosoever believeth in Him should not perish but have eternal life" (John 3:14–15). In these words, Christ makes a comparison on this manner: When anyone of the Israelites were stung to death by fiery serpents, his cure was not by any physick[16] or surgery, but only by the casting of his eyes up to the brazen serpent, which Moses had erected by God's commandment. Even so, in the cure of our souls, when we are stung to death by sin, there is nothing required within us for our recovery but only that we cast up and fix the eye of our faith on Christ and His righteousness.

Reason 2. The *exclusive forms* of speech used in Scripture prove thus much: We are justified freely, not of the law, not by the law, without the law, without works, not of works, not according to works, not of us, not by the works of the law, but by faith. [Gal. 2:16]. "All boasting excluded, only believe" (Luke 8:50). These distinctions, whereby works and the law are excluded in the work of justification, do include thus much, that faith alone justifies.

Reason 3. Very reason may teach thus much, for no gift in man is apt and fit as a spiritual hand to receive and apply Christ and His righteousness unto a sinner, but faith. Indeed love, hope, the fear of God, and repentance have their several uses in men, but none serve for this end to apprehend Christ and His merits. None of them all have this receiving property, and therefore there is nothing in man that justifies as a cause but faith alone.

Reason 4. The judgment of the ancient church. Ambrose on Romans 4: "They are blessed to whom *without any labor or work done*, iniquities are remitted and sin covered. *No works of repentance* [are] required of them, but *only that they believe*." And *c.* 3. "Neither working anything, nor requiring the like, are they justified *by faith alone* through the gift of God." And 1 Corinthians 1: "This is appointed of God, that whosever believes in Christ, shall be saved without any work *by faith alone*, freely receiving remission of sins." Austin,[17] "There is *one* propitiation

16. *Physick:* medicine.

17. *Austin*: Augustine.

for all sins, to believe in Christ."[18] Hesychius on Levit. *lib.* 1. *c.* 2, "Grace which is of mercy is *apprehended by faith alone,* and not of works."

Bernard, "Whosoever is pricked for his sins, and thirsts after righteousness, let him believe in Thee, who justifies the sinner; and being justified *by faith alone,* he shall have peace with God."[19] Chrysostom on Galatians 3: "They said, he which rests on faith alone is cursed, but Paul shows, that he is blessed which rests *on faith alone.*" Basil. *de Humil.*, "Let man acknowledge himself to want true justice and that he is justified *only by faith in Christ.*" Origen, on Romans 3: "We think that a man is justified by faith without the works of the law; and he says, that justification by faith alone suffices so as a man, only believing, may be justified." And, "Therefore it lies upon us—to search who was justified by faith without works. And for an example, I think upon the thief, who being crucified with Christ cried unto him, 'Lord remember me when thou comest into thy kingdom'; and there is *no other good work* of his mentioned in the gospel. But for this alone faith, Jesus says unto him, 'This night thou shalt be with me in paradise.'"

III. Difference

The third difference about justification is concerning this point, namely, how far forth good works are required.

The doctrine of the Church of Rome is that there be two kinds of justification: the first and the second, as I have said. The first is when one of an evil man is made a good man; and in this works are wholly excluded, in being wholly of grace. The second is when a man of a just man is made more just; and this they will have to proceed from works of grace, for (say they) as a man when he is once born can by eating and drinking make himself a bigger

18. In the margin: *De verbis dom. serm.* 40.

19. In the margin: *Super Cant. serm.* 22.

man, though he could not at the first make himself a man, even so, a sinner having his first justification may afterward by grace make himself more just. Therefore, they hold these two things: 1. That good works are meritorious causes of the second justification, which they term "actual." 2. That good works are [a] means to increase the first justification, which they call "habitual."

Now let us see how far forth we must join with them in this point. Our consent therefore stands in three conclusions.

Consent 1. That good works done by them that are justified do please God, and are approved of Him, and therefore have a reward.

Consent 2. Good works are necessary to salvation two ways: first, not as causes thereof, either *conversant*, *adjuvant*, or *procreant*, but only as consequents of faith in that they are inseparable companions and fruits of that faith which is indeed necessary to salvation. Second, they are necessary as marks in a way, and as the way itself directing us unto eternal life.

Consent 3. We hold and believe that the righteous man is in some sort justified by works, for so the Holy Ghost speaks plainly and truly that, "Abraham was justified by works" (James 2:21). Thus far we join with them. And the very difference is this: They say we are justified by works, as by causes thereof. We say that we are justified by works as by signs and fruits of our justification before God, and no otherwise. And in this sense must the place of Saint James be understood: that Abraham was justified—that is, declared and made manifest to be just indeed by his obedience, and that even before God. Now that our doctrine is the truth it will appear by reasons on both parts.

Our Reasons

Reason 1. "We conclude that a man is justified by faith without the works of the law" (Rom. 3:28). Some answer that ceremonial works be excluded here; some, that moral works; some, works going before faith. But let them devise what they can for themselves. The truth is that Paul excludes all works whatsoever, as by the very text will appear. For [in] v. 24, he says, "We are justified *freely* by his grace," that is, by the mere gift of God, giving us to understand that a sinner in his justification is merely passive—that is, doing nothing on his part whereby God should accept him to life everlasting. And v. 27, he says, justification by faith "excludes all boasting," and therefore all kind of works are thereby excluded; and specially such as are most of all the matter of boasting, that is, good works. For if a sinner, after that he is justified by the merit of Christ, were justified more by his own works then might he have some matter of boasting in himself. And that we may not doubt of Paul's meaning, consider and read Ephesians 2:8–9: "By grace," says he, "you are saved through faith, and that not of yourselves: it is the gift of God, not of works, lest any man should boast himself." Here Paul excludes all and every work and, directly, works of grace themselves, as appears by the reason following, "For we are his workmanship *created* in Christ Jesus *unto good works*; *which God hath ordained* that we should walk in them." Now let the papists tell me, what be the works which God has prepared for men to walk in, and to which they are regenerate, unless they be the most excellent works of grace? And let them mark how Paul excludes them wholly from the work of justification and salvation.

Reason 2. "If ye be circumcised, ye are bound to the whole law, and ye are abolished from Christ" (Gal. 5:3). Here Paul disputes against such men as would be saved partly by Christ, and partly by the works of the law. Hence, I reason thus: If any man will be justified by works, he is bound to fulfill the whole law, according to the rigor thereof; that is Paul's ground. I now assume: no man can fulfill the law according to the rigor thereof—for the lives and works of the most righteous men are imperfect, and stained with sin—and therefore they are taught every day to say on this manner, "forgive us our debts" (Matt. 6:12). Again, our knowledge is imperfect, and therefore our faith, repentance, and sanctification is answerable. And lastly, the regenerate man is partly flesh and partly spirit; and therefore, his best works are partly from the flesh and in part only spiritual. Thus then, for any man to be bound to the rigor of the whole law is as much as if he were bound to his own damnation.

Reason 3. Election to salvation is of grace without works; therefore, the justification of a sinner is of grace alone without works. For it is a certain rule that the cause of a cause is the cause of a thing caused. Now grace without works is the cause of election, which election is the cause of our justification. And therefore, grace without works is the cause of justification.

Reason 4. A man must first be fully justified before he can do a good work; for the person must first please God before his works can please Him. But the person of a sinner cannot please God until he be perfectly justified. And therefore, until he be justified, he cannot do so much as one good work. And thus, good works cannot be any meritorious causes of justification—after which they are—both for time and order of nature. In a word, whereas they make two distinct justifications, we acknowledge that there be degrees of sanctification. Yet so as justification is only one, standing in remission of sins, and God's acceptation of us to life everlasting by Christ; and this justification has no degrees but is perfect at the very first.

Objections of Papists

Objection 1. "Judge me according to my righteousness" (Ps. 7:8). Hence, they reason thus: If David be judged according to his righteousness, then may he be justified thereby; but David desires to be judged according to his righteousness, and therefore he was justified thereby. *Answer.* There be two kinds of righteousness: one of the person; the other of the cause or action. The righteousness of a man's person is whereby it is accepted into the favor of God unto life eternal. The righteousness of the action or cause is, when the action or cause is judged of God to be good and just. Now David, in this psalm, speaks only of the righteousness of the action, or innocency of his cause, in that he was falsely charged to have sought the kingdom. In like manner, it is said of Phineas, that his act in killing Zimri and Cosbie, "was imputed to him for righteousness" (Ps. 106:31); not because it was a satisfaction to the law, the rigor whereof could not be fulfilled in that one work; but because God accepted of it as a just work, and as a token of his righteousness and zeal for God's glory.

Objection 2. The Scripture says in sundry places that men are blessed which do good works. "Blessed is the man that is upright in heart, and walketh in the law of the Lord" (Ps. 119:1). *Answer.* The man is blessed that endeavors to keep God's commandments. Yet is he not blessed simply because he does so, but because he is in Christ, by whom he does so—and his obedience to the law of God is a sign thereof.

Objection 3. When man confesses his sins and humbles himself by prayer and fasting, God's wrath is pacified and stayed; therefore, prayer and fasting are causes of justification before God. *Answer.* Indeed, men that truly humble themselves by prayer and fasting do appease the wrath of God. Yet not properly by these actions, but by their faith expressed and testified in them, whereby they apprehend that which appeases God's wrath—even the merits of Christ—in whom the Father is well pleased, and for whose sake alone He is well pleased with us.

Objection 4. Sundry persons in Scripture are commended for perfection, as Noah, and Abraham, Zachariah, and Elizabeth. And Christ bids us all to be perfect; and where there is any perfection of works, there also works may justify. *Answer.* There be two kinds of perfection: perfection in parts and perfection in degrees. Perfection in parts is when, being regenerate and having the seeds of all necessary virtues, we endeavor accordingly to obey God, not in some few, but in all and every part of the law, as Josias turned unto God according to all the law of Moses. Perfection in degrees is when a man keeps every commandment of God, and that according to the rigor thereof, in the very highest degree. Now then, whereas we are commanded to be perfected, and have examples of the same perfection in Scripture, both commandments and examples must be understood of perfection in parts and of perfection in degrees, which cannot be attained unto in this life; though we for our parts must daily strive to come as near [unto] it as possibly we can.

Objection 5. "Our momentary afflictions work in us a greater measure of glory" (2 Cor. 4:17). Now if afflictions work our salvation, then works also do the same. *Answer.* Afflictions work salvation, not as causes procuring it, but as means directing us thereto. And thus also must we esteem of works in the matter of our salvation, as of a certain way or a mark therein, directing us to glory, not causing and procuring it. As Bernard says, they are *via Regni, non causa regnandi.* "The way to the kingdom, not the cause of reigning there."[20]

Objection 6. We are justified by the same thing whereby we are judged; but we are judged by our good works, therefore justified also. *Answer.* The proposition is false; for judgment is an act of God, declaring a man to be just that is already just. And justification is another distinct act of God, whereby He makes him to be just that is by nature unjust. And therefore, in equity the last judgment is to proceed by works, because they are the fittest

20. In the margin: *Lib. de grat. & lib. arbit.*

means to make trial of every man's cause and serve fitly to declare whom God has justified in this life.

Objection 7. Wicked men are condemned for evil works; and therefore, righteous men are justified by good works. *Answer.* The reason holds not, for there is great difference between evil and good works. An evil work is perfectly evil, and so deserves damnation. But there is no good work of any man that is perfectly good, and therefore cannot justify.

Objection 8. To believe in Christ is a work, and by it we are justified; and if one work do justify, why may we not be justified by all the works of the law? *Answer.* Faith must be considered two ways: first, as a work, quality, or virtue: second, as an instrument, or [a] hand reaching out itself to receive Christ's merit. And we are justified by faith, not as it is a work, virtue, or quality, but as it is an instrument to receive and apply that thing whereby we are justified. And therefore, it is a figurative speech to say, "We are justified by faith." Faith considered by itself makes no man righteous—neither does the action of faith, which is to apprehend, justify—but the object of faith, which is Christ's obedience apprehended.

These are the principal reasons commonly used, which as we see are of no moment. To conclude therefore, we hold that works concur to justification, and that we are justified thereby as by signs and effects, not as causes; for both the beginning, middle, and accomplishment of our justification is only in Christ. And hereupon John says, "If any man (being already justified) sin, we have an advocate with the Father, Jesus Christ,... and He is the propitiation for our sins" (1 John 2:1–2). And to make our good works means, or causes of our justification, is to make every man a savior to himself.

THE FIFTH POINT

Of Merits

By "merit" we understand anything or any work, whereby God's favor and life everlasting is procured; and that for the dignity and excellency of the work or thing done, or a good work done, binding him that receives it to repay the like.

I. Our Consent

Touching merits, we consent in two conclusions with them: The first conclusion, that merits are so far forth necessary, that without them there can be no salvation. The second, that Christ our Mediator and Redeemer is the root and fountain of all merit.

II. The Dissent or Difference

The popish church places merits within man, making two sorts thereof: the merit of the person and the merit of the work. The merit of the person is a dignity in the person whereby it is worthy of life everlasting. And this (as they say) is to be found in infants dying after baptism who, though they want good works, yet are they not void of this kind of merit, for which they receive the kingdom of heaven. The merit of the work is a dignity or excellency in the work whereby it is made fit and enabled to deserve life everlasting for the doer. And works (as they teach) are meritorious two ways: first, by covenant, because God has made a promise of reward unto them; second, by their own dignity, for Christ has merited that our works might merit. And this is the substance of their doctrine.[1]

From it we dissent in these points: 1. We renounce all personal merits, that is, all merits within the person of any mere man. 2. And we renounce all merit of works, that is, all merit of any work done by any mere man whatsoever. And the true merit—whereby we look to attain the favor of God and life everlasting—is to be found in the Person of Christ alone, who is the storehouse of all our merits, [and] whose prerogative it is to be the person alone in whom God is well pleased. God's favor is of infinite dignity, and no creature is able to do a work that may countervail the favor of God, save Christ alone, who by reason of the dignity of His Person—being not a mere man but God-man, or Man-God—can do such works as are of endless dignity, everyway answerable to the favor of God, and therefore sufficient to merit the same for us. And though a merit or meritorious work agree only to the Person of Christ, yet is it made ours by imputation. For as His righteousness is made ours, so are His merits depending thereon; but His righteousness is made ours by imputation, as I have shown. Hence arises another point, namely, that as Christ's righteousness is made ours really by imputation to make us righteous, so we, by the merit of His righteousness imputed to us, do merit and deserve life everlasting. And this is our doctrine. In a word, the papist maintains the merits of his own works, but we renounce them all and rest only on the merit of Christ. And that our doctrine is truth, and theirs [is] falsehood,

1. This paragraph break is not in the original.

I will make manifest by sundry reasons, and then answer their arguments to the contrary.

Our Reasons

Reason 1. The first shall be taken from the properties and conditions that must be in a work meritorious, and they are four: 1. A man must do it of himself, and by himself; for if it be done by another, the merit does not properly belong to the doer. 2. A man must do it of his own free will and pleasure, not of due debt; for when we do that which we are bound to do, we do no more but our duty.

The work must be done to the profit of another, who thereupon must be bound to repay the like. 4. The reward and the work must be in proportion equal; for if the reward be more than the work, it is not a reward of desert but a gift of good will. Hence follows a notable conclusion: That Christ's manhood considered apart from His Godhead cannot merit at God's hand, though it be more excellent every way than all, both men and angels. For being thus considered, it does nothing of itself, but by grace received from the Godhead; though it be also without measure. Second, Christ's manhood is a creature, and in that regard bound to do whatsoever it does. Third, Christ, as man, cannot give anything to God but that which He received from God; therefore cannot the manhood properly, by itself, merit, but only as it is personally united to the Godhead of the Son. And if this be so, then much less can any mere man or any angel merit. Yes, it is a madness to think, that either our actions or persons should be capable of any merit whereby we might attain to life eternal.

Reason 2. "*And show mercy* upon thousands in them that love me and keep my commandments" (Ex. 20:6). Hence, I reason thus: where reward is given upon mercy, there is no merit; but reward is given of mercy to them that fulfill the law, therefore no merit. What can we any way deserve, when our full recompense must be of mercy? And this appears further by Adam: If he had stood to this day, he could not by his continual and perfect obedience have procured a further increase of favor at God's hand but should only have continued [in] that happy estate in which he was first created.

Reason 3. Scripture directly condemns merit of works. "The wages of sin is death: but *the gift of God* is eternal life through Jesus Christ our Lord" (Rom. 6:23). The proposition of the argument required that S. Paul should have said: The reward of good works is eternal life, if life everlasting could be deserved, which cannot, because it is a free gift. Again, "We are saved, not by works of righteousness which we have done, but according to his mercy he saved us" (Titus 3:5). And "By grace you are saved through faith, and that not of yourselves, it is the gift of God; not of works, which God hath prepared that we should walk in them" (Eph. 2:8, 10). If any works be crowned, it is certain that the sufferings of martyrs shall be rewarded. Now of them, Paul says, "The sufferings of this life *are not worthy* of the glory to come" (Rom. 8:18). Where then is the value and dignity of others' works? To this purpose, Ambrose says, "The just man, though he be tormented in the brazen bull,[2] is still just, because he justifies God and says, *he suffers* less than his sins deserve."

Reason 4. Whosoever will merit, must fulfill the whole law. But none can keep the whole law, "for if we say, we have no sin, we deceive ourselves" (1 John 1:8). And he that sins against one commandment is guilty of the whole law [James 2:10]. And what can he merit that is guilty of the breach of the whole law?

---

2. *Brazen bull:* a torture and execution device designed in ancient Greece.

Reason 5. We are taught to pray on this manner, "Give us this day our daily bread" (Matt. 6:11). Wherein we acknowledge every morsel of bread to be the mere gift of God without desert; and therefore, must we much more acknowledge life eternal to be every way the gift of God. It must needs therefore be a satanical insolency for any man to imagine that he can by his works merit eternal life, who cannot merit bread.

Reason 6. Consent of the ancient church. Bernard, "Those which we call our merits are the way to the kingdom and not *the cause of reigning.*"[3] Augustine, *Manuel*, *chap.* 22, "All my hope is in the death of my Lord. His death was my merit. My *merit is the passion of the Lord.* I shall not be void of merits, so long as God's mercies are not wanting." Basil on Psalm 114: "Eternal rest is reserved for them which have striven lawfully in this life; not *for the merits* of their doings, but upon the grace of the most bountiful God, in which they trusted." Augustine on Psalm 120: "He crowns you, because He crowns His own gifts, not your merits." And Psalm 142: "Lord, Thou wilt quicken me in Thy justice, not in mine; not because I deserved it, but because thou hast compassion."

III. Objections of Papists

Objection 1. In sundry places of Scripture, promise of reward is made to them that believe and do good works. Therefore, our works do merit; for a reward and merit be relatives. *Answer.* Reward is twofold: of debt and of mercy. Life everlasting is not a reward of debt, but of mercy, given of the good will of God without anything done of man. Second, the kingdom of heaven is properly an inheritance given of a father to a child; and therefore, it is called a reward, not properly, but by a figure or by resemblance. For as a workman, having ended his labor, receives his wages,

3. In the margin: *De interpellatione David.* 4 *vel. Ps.* 72.

so after men have led their lives and finished their course in keeping faith and good conscience, as dutiful children, God gives them eternal life. And hereupon it is termed a reward. Third, if I should grant that life everlasting is a deserved reward, it is not for our works, but for Christ's merit imputed to us, causing us thereby to merit. And thus, the relation stands directly between the *reward* and Christ's *merit* applied unto us.

Objection 2. Christ, by His death, merited that our works should merit life everlasting. *Answer.* That is false. All we find in Scripture is that Christ, by His merit, procured pardon of sin, imputation of righteousness, and life everlasting. And it is nowhere said in the Word of God that Christ did merit that our works should merit. It is a dotage of their own devising. He died not for our good works to make them able to satisfy God's anger, but for our sins that they might be pardoned. Thus much says the Scripture, and no more. And in that Christ did sufficiently merit life eternal for us, by His own death, it is a sufficient proof that He never intended to give us power of meriting the same, unless we suppose that at some time He gives more than is needful. Again, Christ in the office of mediation as He is a King, Priest, and Prophet, admits no deputy or fellow. For He is a most perfect Mediator, doing all things by Himself without the help of any. And the ministers that dispense the Word are not His deputies, but reasonable and voluntary instruments which He uses. But if men by works can merit increase of grace and happiness for themselves, then Christ has partners in the work of redemption—men doing that by Him, which He does of Himself, in procuring their salvation. No, if this might stand that Christ did merit that our works should merit, then Christ should merit that our stained righteousness being for this cause not capable of merit should nevertheless merit.

I call it stained because we are partly flesh and partly spirit, and therefore in ourselves deserving the curse of the law, though we be regenerate. Again, for one good work we do, we have many evil, the offence whereof defaces the merit of our best deeds and makes them too light in the balance of the law.

Objection 3. Our works merit by bargain or covenant, because God has promised to reward them. *Answer.* The Word of God sets down two covenants: one legal, the other evangelical. In the legal covenant, life everlasting is promised to works—for that is the condition of the law: do these things and you shall live. But on this manner can no man merit life everlasting, because none is able to do all that the law requires, whether we respect the manner or the measure of obedience. In the evangelical covenant, the promises that are made are not made to any work or virtue in man, but to the worker—not for any merit of his own person or work, but for the Person and merit of Christ. For example, it is a promise of the gospel, "Be faithful unto death, and I will give thee the crown of life" (Rev. 2:10). Here the promise is not made to the virtue of fidelity but to the faithful person, whose fidelity is but a token that he is in Christ, for the merit of whose obedience God promises the crown of life. And therefore, Christ says further: "I come quickly, and will give to every man according to his works" (Rev. 22:12). Mark, he says not to the work or for the work, but to the worker according to his works. And thus, the bond of all other promises of the gospel, in which God willingly binds Himself to reward our works, do not directly concern us, but have respect to the Person and obedience of Christ, for whose sake alone God binds Himself as debtor unto us and gives the recompense or reward, according to the measure of our faith testified by our works. And therefore, it cannot be truly gathered that works do merit by any promise or covenant passed on God's part to man. Some may say, "If works merit not, why are they mentioned in the promise?" I answer, not because they merit, but because they are tokens, that the doer of the works is in Christ, for whose merit the promise shall be accomplished.

Objection 4. Good works are perfect and without fault, for they are the works of the Holy Ghost, who cannot sin. Therefore, they merit. *Answer.* If works did proceed only and immediately from the Holy Ghost, there could not be any fault in them. But our works come from the Holy Ghost, in and by the will and understanding of man. And by this means they are tainted with sin, as water in the fountain is both clear and sweet, yet the streams thereof passing through the filthy channel are defiled thereby. Again, they reason thus: That which we are bound to do has no fault in it; but we are bound to do good works, therefore, they are perfect. *Answer.* The proposition must be expounded: that which we are bound to do, in itself, according to the intention of the commander, has no fault. Or, that which we are bound to do according as we are bound to do it, has no fault, yet in regard of the intention of the doer, or in regard of our manner of doing, it may be faulty.

Objection 5. Christ says that the faithful in the church of Sardis "shall walk with him in white, for they are worthy" (Rev. 3:4); therefore, believers merit. *Answer.* Every believer is worthy to walk with Christ, yet not worthy in himself, but in Christ, to whom he is united and made bone of His bone and flesh of His flesh. And by reason of this conjunction it is, that men are said to be worthy because they are enriched with Christ's merits and righteousness.

Objection 6. Everlasting life is termed "a crown," and "a crown of righteousness to be given of a just judge" (2 Tim. 4:8); therefore, man for his part—by his works—deserves the same. *Answer.* Everlasting life is called a crown only in resemblance. For as he which runs a race must continue and run to the end and then be crowned, even so must we continue to walk in good works unto the end and then receive eternal life. And it is called a crown of righteousness, not because it belongs to any man by due and desert, but because God has bound Himself by a promise to give it, in performing whereof He is termed just. And by virtue of this promise it is obtained and no otherwise. These are the principal objections, by which we may judge what the rest are. And thus we see what is the truth, namely, that merit is necessary to salvation; yet neither merit of man's work or person but the merit of Christ imputed to us, whereby we, being in Him, do procure and deserve the favor of God and life eternal.

THE SIXTH POINT

Of Satisfaction

I. Our Consent

Conclusion 1. First, we acknowledge and hold civil or politic[1] satisfaction, that is, a recompense for injuries and damages offered any way to our neighbors. This Zacchaeus practiced, when at his conversion he restored fourfold things gotten by forged cavillation.[2] Again, by civil satisfaction I understand the imposition of fines, mulcts,[3] and penalties upon offenders, and the inflicting of death upon malefactors. For all these are satisfactions to the law and societies of men when they are wronged. All these we maintain as necessary, for neither church nor commonwealth can be without them, considering they are notable means to uphold civil peace; and otherwhiles they are fruits of true faith, as the satisfaction of Zacchaeus was.

Conclusion 2. We acknowledge canonical or ecclesiastical satisfaction. And that is when any having given offence to the church

1. *Politic:* judicious.

2. *Cavillation*: taking advantage of technical flaws in order to defraud; chicanery or trickery.

3. *Mulct*: a compulsory payment or an unfair tax.

of God or any part thereof, do make an open, public testimony of their repentance. Miriam, for murmuring against Moses [Numbers 12], was stricken with leprosy, and afterward by his prayer she was cleansed—and yet for all that she must go seven days out of the tents and congregation that she might make a kind of satisfaction to the people for her trespass. And in the Old Testament, sackcloth and ashes were signs of their satisfaction.

Conclusion 3. We hold that no man can be saved, unless he make a perfect satisfaction to the justice of God for all his sins—because God is infinite in justice, and therefore will either exact an everlasting punishment or satisfaction for the same.

II. The Dissent or Difference

The points of our difference and dissent are these. The Church of Rome teaches and believes that Christ by His death has made a satisfaction for all the sins of men, and for the eternal punishment of them all—yet so, as they themselves must satisfy the justice of God for the temporal punishment of the offences, either on earth or in purgatory. We teach and believe that Christ, by His death and passion, has made a perfect and all-sufficient satisfaction to the justice of God for all the sins of men, and for the whole punishment thereof, both eternal and temporal. Thus we differ, and herein we, for our parts, must forever stand at difference with them—so as if there were no more points of variance but this one, it should be sufficient to keep us always from uniting our religions, and cause us to obey the voice of Christ, "Come out of her, my people" (Rev. 18:4). For as in the former points, so in this also, the papists err, not in circumstance, but in the very foundation and life of religion.

Our Reasons

Reason 1. A satisfaction that is made imperfectly, either directly or by consequent, is indeed no satisfaction at all. But the papists make Christ's satisfaction imperfect in that they do add a supply by human satisfactions. And thus much a learned schoolman, Biel, in plain words confessed, "Although," says he, "the passion of Christ be the principal merit for which grace is conferred, the opening of the kingdom and glory, *yet is it never the alone and total meritorious cause.* It is manifest, because always with the merit of Christ there concurs some work, as the merit of congruity or condignity of him that receives grace or glory, if he be of years and have the use of reason, or of some other for him if he want reason."[4] For that which admits a supply by another is imperfect in itself. Therefore, human satisfactions cannot stand. Learned papists make answer that Christ's satisfaction and man's may stand well together. "For," say they, "Christ's satisfaction is sufficient in itself to answer the justice of God for all sin and punishment, but it is not sufficient to this or that man until it be applied. And it must be applied by our satisfaction made to God for the temporal punishment of our sins." But I say again, that man's satisfaction can be no means to apply the satisfaction of Christ, and I prove it thus: The means of applying God's blessings and graces unto man are twofold: some respect God Himself and some respect man. Those which respect God are such whereby God, on His part, offers and conveys His mercies in Christ unto man. Of this sort are the preaching of the Word, baptism, and the Lord's Supper—and these are as it were the hand of God whereby He reaches down and gives unto us Christ with all His benefits. The other means of applying on man's part are those whereby the said benefits are received. Of this sort, there is only one, namely faith, whereby we

4. In the margin: *Super lib.* 3. *dict.* 19. *conclus.* 5.

believe that Christ, with all His benefits, belongs unto us. And that is the hand of man whereby he receives Christ as He is offered or exhibited by God in the Word and sacraments. As for other means beside these, in Scripture we find none. Foolish therefore is the answer of the papists that make men's satisfactions means to apply the satisfaction of Christ unto us. For by human satisfactions, Christ is neither offered on God's part, nor yet received on man's part. Let them prove it if they can.[5]

Others, not content with this their former answer, say that our satisfactions do nothing derogate from the satisfaction of Christ, because our works have their dignity and merit from Christ's satisfaction, He meriting that our works should satisfy God's justice for temporal punishment. But this is also absurd and false, as the former was. For if Christ did satisfy that man might satisfy, then Christ makes every believer to be a Christ, a Jesus, a Redeemer, and a Priest in the same order with His own self. But to make sinful man his own redeemer, though it be but from temporal punishments, is a doctrine of devils. For the Holy Ghost teaches that the priesthood of Christ is incommunicable and cannot pass from Him to any other [Heb. 7:24]. Now to make satisfaction for sin, or any part of the punishment thereof, is a duty or a part of Christ's priesthood; and therefore, to make satisfaction is a work that cannot pass from His person to the person of any man. Again, if Christ by His satisfaction give[s] power to man to satisfy, then man satisfies by Christ, and Christ besides His own satisfaction upon the cross must daily satisfy in man to the end of the world. But this cannot be, for Christ upon the cross, when death was upon Him, said, "It is finished" (John 19:30), that is, "I have fully satisfied for all the sins of mankind, both in respect of the fault and punishment." As for

5. This paragraph break is not the original.

Christ's burial and resurrection which followed His death, they served not to satisfy, but to confirm and ratify[6] the same. Again, Paul says, "He that knew no sin was made *sin for us*" (2 Cor. 5:21), that is, the punishment of sin for us. But if the Church of Rome say true that Christ daily satisfies, then Paul spoke too short, and should have said further, that "Christ was made *sin for us, and in us too*"— and that God was not only in Christ, but also in us, reconciling the world to Himself. But Paul never knew this learning, and therefore let them turn themselves which way they will, by putting a supplement to Christ's satisfaction, they do indeed annihilate the same.

Reason 2. In sundry places of Scripture, especially in the Epistles of Paul, we are said to be redeemed, justified, and saved *freely*. Which word, *freely*, imports that we are justified and saved without anything done on our part or by ourselves in the matter of our salvation. And if this be so, then can we do nothing at all that may satisfy the justice of God for the least punishment of our sins. If we satisfy in our own persons, we are not saved freely; and if we be saved freely, we make no satisfaction at all.

Reason 3. We pray daily, "forgive us our sins" (Luke 11:4). Now to plead pardon, and to satisfy for our sins, be contrary. And for all things for which we can make satisfaction, we need not crave a pardon; but we are taught in the foresaid petition wholly and only to use the plea of pardon for our sins, and therefore we acknowledge that we cannot make any satisfaction at all.

Reason 4. The judgment of the ancient church. Tertullian in *de Baptism*, "Guiltiness being taken away, the *punishment is also taken away*." Augustine: "Christ, by taking upon Him the punishment and not the fault, has done away both the fault and *the punishment*."[7] And [in] *Tom.* 10 *hom.* 5, he says, "when we are gone

6. The words *and ratify* are not in the 1635 edition.

7. In the margin: *Serm.* 37. *de verb. Apost.*

out of this world, there will remain no compunction or satisfaction." Some new editions have foisted in the word *aliqua,* and so have turned the sense on this manner: "There will remain no compunction or some satisfaction." But that is flat against Augustine's meaning, who says a little before, "that when the way is ended there is no compounding of our cause with any." Chrysostom [in] *proem. in Esa.*, "Say not to me, I have sinned. How shall I be freed from so many sins? You cannot; but your God can. Yes, and He will so blot out your sins that there shall *remain no print of them.* Which thing befalls not to the body, for when it is healed there remains a scar, but God, as soon as He exempts you from punishment, He gives the justice." Ambrose says, "I read of Peter's tears, but I read not *of his satisfaction.*"[8] Again, "Let us adore Christ, that He may say unto us, 'Fear not the sins of this world, nor the waves of bodily sufferings. I have remission of sins.'" Jerome says in Psalm 31: "The sin that is covered is not seen, the sin that is not seen is not imputed, that which is *not imputed is not punished.*" Chrysostom in Matthew *homil.* 44: "Among all men, some endure punishment in this life, and the life to come; others in this life alone, others alone in the life to come, others neither in this life, nor the life to come. There alone, as Dives, who was not lord so much as one drop of water. Here alone, the incestuous man among the Corinthians. Neither here nor there, as the apostles and prophets, as also Job and the rest of this kind. For they endured *no sufferings for punishment*, but that they might be known to be conquerors in this fight."

III. Objections of Papists

Objection 1. [Leviticus 4.] Moses, according to God's commandment, prescribed several sacrifices for several persons; and they were means of satisfaction for the temporal punishments of their

8. In the margin: Luke 22. *Petri negat. de bono mor.*

daily sins. *Answer.* Those sacrifices were only signs and types of Christ's satisfaction to be offered to His Father in His alone sacrifice upon the cross. And whosoever offered any sacrifice in the Old Testament did thus and no otherwise esteem of it but as a type and figure of better things. Second, the said sacrifices were satisfactions to the church, whereby men did testify their repentance for their offences, and likewise their desire to be reconciled to God and men. And such kind of satisfactions we acknowledge.

Objection 2. Men, whose sins are all pardoned, have afterward sundry crosses and afflictions laid upon them unto the end of their days. Therefore, in all likelihood they make satisfaction to God for temporal punishments. As for example, the Israelites for murmuring against the Lord in the wilderness were all barred from the land of promise. And the like befell Moses and Aaron for not glorifying God, as they should have done at the waters of strife. *Answer.* Man must be considered in a twofold estate, as he is under the law, and as he is under grace. In the first estate, all afflictions are curses or legal punishments, be they little or great. But to them that are in the second estate and believe in Christ, though the same afflictions remain, yet do they change their habit or condition, and are the actions of a Father—serving to be trials, corrections, preventings, admonitions. "When we are judged, we are nurtured of the Lord" (1 Cor. 11:32). And, "If ye endure chastisement, God offereth Himself unto you as children" (Heb. 12:7). And Chrysostom says, 1 Cor. *hom.* 28: "When we are corrected of the Lord, it is more for our admonition than damnation, more for a medicine than for a punishment, more for a correction than for a penalty." And whereas God denied the believing Israelites, with Moses and Aaron, to enter into the land of Canaan, it cannot be proved that it was a punishment or penalty of the law upon them. The Scripture says no more but that it was an admonition to all men in all ages following to take heed of like offences, as Paul writes, "All these things came unto them for ensamples, and were written for our admonition" (1 Cor. 10:11).

Objection 3. David was punished after his repentance for his adultery, for the child died, and he was plagued in his own kind, in the incest of Absalom. And when he had numbered the people he was yet punished in the death of his people after his own repentance. *Answer.* I answer as before, that the hand of God was upon David after his repentance. But yet the judgments which befell him were not curses unto him properly, but corrections for his sins and trials of his faith and means to prevent further sin and to renew both his faith and repentance—as also they served to admonish others in like case. For David was a public person and his sins were offensive, both within the church of God and without.

Objection 4. The prophets of God, when the people are threatened with the plague, famine, sword, captivity, etc., exhorted them to repent and to humble themselves in sackcloth and ashes—and thereby they turned away the wrath of God that was then coming forth against them. Therefore, by temporal humiliation, men may escape the temporal punishments of the Lord. *Answer.* Famine, sword, banishment, the plague, and other judgments sent on God's people, were not properly punishments of sin, but only the corrections of a father whereby He humbled them that they might repent. Or thus, they were punishments tending to correction, not serving for satisfaction. And the punishments of God are turned from them, not because they satisfy the justice of God in their own sufferings, but because by faith they lay hold on the satisfaction of the Messiah and testify the same by their humiliation and repentance.

Objection 5. Daniel gives this counsel to Nebuchadnezzar, "Redeem thy sins by justice, and thine iniquities by alms deeds" (Dan. 4:27). "Behold," say they, "alms deeds are made a means to satisfy for man's iniquities." *Answer.* The word which they translate to "redeem" (as the most learned in the Chaldean tongue with one consent avouch) properly signifies to "break off," as if the prophet should say: "O King, you are a mighty Monarch, and to enlarge your kingdom you have used much injustice and cruelty. Therefore now, repent of your iniquity, and break off these your sins, testify your repentance by doing justice, and give alms to the poor whom you have oppressed." Therefore, here is nothing spoken of satisfaction for sin, but only of testification of repentance by the fruits thereof.

Objection 6. "'Do penance; and bring forth fruits worthy of penance' (Matt. 3:8), which," say they, "are works of satisfaction enjoined by the priest." *Answer.* This text is abused, for the word μετανοεῖτε signifies thus much, "*change your minds* from sin to God," and testify it by good works, that is, by doing the duties of the moral law; which must be done, not because they are means to satisfy God's justice for man's sin, but because they are fruits of that faith and repentance which lies in the heart.

Objection 7. [2 Cor. 7:11.] Paul sets down sundry fruits of repentance, whereof the last is *revenge*, whereby repentant persons punish themselves, thereby to satisfy God's justice for the temporal punishment of their sins. *Answer.* A repentant sinner must take revenge on himself, and that is only to use all means which serve to subdue the corruption of nature, to bridle carnal affections, and to mortify sin; and these kinds of actions are *restrainments* properly, and not punishments, and are directed against the sin, and not against the person.

Lastly, they make three works of satisfaction—prayer, fasting, and alms deeds. For the first, it is mere foolishness to think that man by prayer can satisfy for his sins. It is all one, as if they had said, that a beggar by asking of alms should deserve his alms, or that a debtor by requesting his creditor to pardon his debt should thereby pay his debt. Second, fasting is a thing indifferent, of the same nature with eating and drinking, and of itself confers nothing to the obtainment of the kingdom of heaven, no more than eating and drinking do. Third and lastly, alms deeds cannot be works of satisfaction for sins. For when we give them as we ought, we do but our duty, whereunto we are bound. And we may as well say that a man, by paying one debt, may discharge another, as to say that by doing his duty he may satisfy God's justice for the punishment of his sins. These we confess be fruits of faith, but yet are they no works of satisfaction. But the only and all-sufficient satisfaction made to God's justice for our sins is to be found in the Person of Christ, being procured by the merit of His death and His obedience. And thus our doctrine touching satisfaction is cleared. And it is to be learned carefully of our common people, because the opinion of human satisfaction is natural and sticks fast in the hearts of natural men. Hereupon when any have sinned and feel touch of conscience any way, their manner is then to perform some outward humiliation and repentance, thinking thereby to stop the mouth of conscience, and by doing some ceremonial duties to appease the wrath of God for their sins. Yes, many think to satisfy God's justice by repeating the creed, the Lord's Prayer, and the Ten Commandments, so foolish are they in this kind.

THE SEVENTH POINT

Of Traditions

Traditions are doctrines delivered from hand to hand, either by word of mouth or by writing, beside the written Word of God.

I. Our Consent

Conclusion 1. We hold that the very Word of God has been delivered by tradition. For first God revealed His will to Adam by word of mouth and renewed the same unto the patriarchs; not by writing, but by speech, by dreams, and other inspirations. And thus, the Word of God went from man to man for the space of two thousand and four hundred years, unto the time of Moses, who was the first penman of Holy Scripture. For as touching the Prophecy of Enoch, we commonly hold it was not penned by Enoch, but by some Jew under his name. And for the space of this time, men worshipped God and held the articles of their faith by tradition, not from men, but immediately from God Himself. And the history of the New Testament (as some say) for eighty years— as some others think for the space of twenty years and more—went from hand to hand by tradition, until penned by the apostles, or being penned by others, was approved by them.

Conclusion 2. We hold that the prophets, our Savior Christ, and His apostles, spoke and did many things good and true which were not written in the Scriptures, but came either to us or to our ancestors only by tradition. As it is said that, "Jannes and Jambres were the magicians that withstood Moses" (2 Tim. 3:8), now in the books of the Old Testament we shall not find them once named, and therefore it is likely that the apostle had their names by tradition or by some writings then extant among the Jews. So, [in] Hebrews 12:21, the author of the epistle records of Moses, that when he saw a terrible sight in Mount Sinai, he said, "I tremble and am afraid," which words are not to be found in all the books of the Old Testament. In the epistle of Jude, mention is made that "the devil strove with Michael the archangel about the body of Moses," which point (as also the former) considering it is not to be found in holy writ, it seems the apostle had it by tradition from the Jews. That the prophet Isaiah was killed with a fuller's club is received for truth but yet not recorded in Scripture; and so likewise that the Virgin Mary lived and died a virgin. And in ecclesiastical writers, many worthy sayings of the apostles and other holy men are recorded and received of us for truth which nevertheless are not set down in the books of the Old or New Testament. And many things we hold for truth not written in the Word, if they be not against the Word.

Conclusion 3. We hold that the church of God has power to prescribe ordinances, rules, or traditions, touching time and place of God's worship and touching order and comeliness to be used in the same. And in this regard, Paul, [in] 1 Corinthians 11:2, commends the church of Corinth for keeping his traditions, and [in] Acts 15:29, the Council at Jerusalem decreed that "the churches of the Gentiles should abstain from blood, and from things strangled." This decree is termed a tradition, and it was in force among them so long as the offence of the Jews remained. And these kind[s] of traditions, whether made by general councils or particular synods, we have care to maintain and observe, these caveats being remembered: first, that they prescribe nothing childish or absurd to be done; second, that they be not imposed as any part of God's worship; third, that they be severed from superstition or opinion of merit; lastly, that the church of God be not burdened with the multitude of them. And thus much touching traditions.

II. The Difference

Papists teach that beside the written Word, there be certain unwritten traditions which must be believed as profitable and necessary to salvation. And these they say are twofold: apostolical, namely such as were delivered by the apostles and not written; and ecclesiastical, which the church decrees as occasion is offered. We hold that the Scriptures are most perfect, containing in them all doctrines needful to salvation, whether they concern faith and manners. And therefore, we acknowledge no such traditions beside the written Word which shall be necessary to salvation so as he which believes them not cannot be saved.

Our Reasons

Testimony 1. "Thou shalt not add to the words that I command thee, nor take anything therefrom" (Deut. 4:2). Therefore, the written Word is sufficient for all doctrines pertaining to salvation. If it be said that this commandment is spoken as well of the unwritten as of the written Word, I answer that Moses speaks of the written Word only. For these few words are a certain preface which he set before a long commentary made of the written law for this end: to make the people more attentive and obedient.

Testimony 2. "To the law and to the testimony. If they speak not according to this word, it is because there is no light in them" (Isa. 8:20). Here the prophet teaches what must be done in cases of difficulty. Men must not run to the wizard or soothsayer, but to the law and testimony. And here he commends the written Word as sufficient to resolve all doubts and scruples in conscience whatsoever.

Testimony 3. "Those things were written that ye might believe that Jesus is the Christ, and in believing might have everlasting life" (John 20:31). Here is set down the full end of the gospel and the whole written Word, which is to bring men to faith, and consequently to salvation. And therefore, the whole Scripture alone is sufficient to this end without traditions. If it be said that this place must be understood of Christ's miracles only, I answer that miracles without the doctrine of Christ and knowledge of His sufferings can bring no man to life everlasting. And therefore, the place must be understood of the doctrine of Christ and not of His miracles alone, as Paul teaches, "If we, or an angel from heaven preach unto you anything *beside that* which we have preached, let him be accursed" (Gal. 1:8). And to this effect he blames them that taught but a divers doctrine to that which he had taught [1 Tim. 1:3].

Testimony 4. "The whole Scripture is given by inspiration of God, and is profitable to teach, to improve, to correct, and to instruct in righteousness, that the man of God may be absolute, being made perfect unto every good work" (2 Tim. 3:16–17). In these words be contained two arguments to prove the sufficiency of Scripture without unwritten verities. The first, that which is profitable to these four uses, namely, to teach all necessary truth, to confute all errors, to correct faults in manners, and to instruct in righteousness—that is, to inform all men in all good duties, that is sufficient to salvation. But Scripture serves for all these uses and therefore it is sufficient, and unwritten traditions are superfluous. The second, that which can make the man of God—that is, prophets, and apostles, and the ministers of the Word—perfect in all the duties of their callings; that same Word is sufficient to make all other men perfect in all good works. But God's Word is able to make the man of God perfect. Therefore, it is sufficient to prescribe the true and perfect way to eternal life without the help of unwritten traditions.

Testimony 5. The judgment of the church. Tertullian says, "Take from heretics the opinions which they maintain with the heathen, that they may defend their questions by *Scripture alone*, and they cannot stand."[1] Again, "We need no curiosity after Christ Jesus, nor inquisition after the gospel. When we believe it, we desire to *believe nothing beside*; for this we first believe that there is nothing *more* which we may believe." Jerome on Matthew 23, writing of an opinion that John the Baptist was killed because he foretold the coming of Christ, says thus: "This, because it has not authority from Scriptures, may as easily be condemned as approved," in which words there is a conclusion with a *minor*, and the *major* is to be supplied by the rules of logic thus: that which has not authority from Scriptures may as easily be condemned as approved. But this opinion is so; therefore. Behold a notable argument against all unwritten traditions. Augustine *book* 2. *cap.* 9. *de doctr. Christian* says, "In those things which are plainly set down in Scripture are found *all those points which contain faith and manners* of living well." Vicentius Lirinen says, "The canon of the Scripture is perfect and fully sufficient in itself *for all things*."

Beside these testimonies, other reasons there be that serve to prove this point:[2]

---

1. In the margin: *De resurrectione carnis.*

2. This paragraph break is not in the original.

Reason 1. The practice of Christ and His apostles, who for the confirmation of the doctrine which they taught used always the testimony of Scripture. Neither can it be proved that they ever confirmed any doctrine by tradition. "I continue unto this day witnessing both to small and great, saying *none other things than those* which the prophets and Moses did say should come" (Acts 26:22). And by this we are given to understand that we must always have recourse to the written Word as being sufficient to instruct us in matters of salvation.[3]

Reason 2. If the believing of unwritten traditions were necessary to salvation, then we must as well believe the writings of the ancient Fathers as the writings of the apostles, because apostolical traditions are not elsewhere to be found but in their books. And we may not believe their sayings as the Word of God, because they often err, being subject to error. And for this cause their authority, when they speak of traditions, may be suspected. And we may not always believe them upon their word.

III. Objections for Traditions

Objection 1. First, they allege 2 Thessalonians 2:15, where the apostle bids that church keep the "ordinances which he taught them either by word or letter." Hence, they gather that beside the written Word, there be unwritten traditions that are indeed necessary to be kept and obeyed. *Answer.* It is very likely that this epistle to the Thessalonians was the first that ever Paul wrote to any church, though in order it have not the first place. And therefore, at that time when this epistle was penned, it might well fall out that some things needful to salvation were delivered by word of mouth, not being as yet written by any apostle. Yet the same things were afterward set down in writing, either in the second epistle or in the epistles of Paul.

3. This paragraph break is not in the original.

Objection 2. That *Scripture is Scripture* is a point to be believed, but that is a tradition unwritten; and therefore, one tradition there is not written that we are to believe. *Answer.* That the books of the Old and New Testament are Scripture, it is to be gathered and believed, not upon bare tradition, but from the very books themselves, on this manner: Let a man that is endowed with the spirit of discerning read the several books; withal let him consider the professed author thereof which is God Himself, and the matter therein contained, which is a most divine and absolute truth full of piety; the manner and form of speech, which is full of majesty in the simplicity of words; the end whereat they wholly aim, which is the honor and glory of God alone, etc., and he shall be resolved that Scripture is Scripture, even by the Scripture itself. Yes, and by this means he may discern any part of Scripture from the writings of men whatsoever. Thus then, Scripture proves itself to be Scripture, and yet we despise not the universal consent or tradition of the church in this case, which though it does not persuade the conscience, yet is it a notable inducement to move us to reverence and regard the writings of the prophets and apostles. It will be said, where is it written that Scripture is Scripture? I answer, not in any one particular place or book of Scripture, but in every line and page of the whole Bible—to him that can read with the spirit of discerning and can discern the voice of the true pastor, as the sheep of Christ can do.

Objection 3. Some books of the canon of the Scripture are lost, as the "book of the wars of God" (Num. 21:14), "The book of the just" (Josh. 10:13), the "book of Chronicles of the kings of Israel" and Judah (1 Kings 14:19), [and] the books of certain prophets: Nathan, Gad, Iddo, Ahiah, and Semiah. And therefore, the matter of these books must come to us by tradition. *Answer*. Though it be granted that some books of canonical Scripture be lost, yet the Scripture still remains sufficient—because the matter of those books (so far forth as it was necessary to salvation) is contained in these books of Scripture that are now extant. Again, I take it to be truth (though some think otherwise) that no part of the canon is lost. For Paul says, "Whatsoever things were written aforetime, were written for our learning that we through patience and comfort of the Scriptures, etc." (Rom. 15:4), where he takes it for granted that the whole canon of Holy Scripture was then extant. For if he had thought that some books of Scripture had been lost, he would have said: "Whatsoever was written and is now extant, was written for our learning and comfort." For books that are lost serve neither for learning nor comfort. Again, to hold that any books of Scripture should be lost, calls into question God's providence, and the fidelity of the church, [which] has the books of God in keeping, and is therefore called the pillar and ground of truth. And touching the books before mentioned, I answer thus: "The book of the wars of God" (Num. 21:14), might be some short bill or narration of things done among the Israelites, which in the days of Moses went from hand to hand. For sometimes a book in Scripture signifies a *roll* or *catalogue*, as the first chapter of Matthew, which contains the genealogy of our Savior Christ, is called "the book of the generation of Jesus Christ" (Matt. 1:1). Again, the "book of the just," and the "books of Chronicles," which are said to be lost, were but as the Chronicles of England are with us—even political records of the acts and events of things in the kingdom of Judah and Israel, out of which the prophets gathered things necessary to be known, and placed them in Holy Scripture. As for the books of Iddo, Ahiah, Semiah, Gad, and Nathan, they are contained in the books of the Kings and Chronicles, and in the books of Samuel, which were not written by him alone, but by sundry prophets [1 Chron. 29:29], as also was the book of Judges. As for the books of Solomon, which are lost, they did not concern religion and matters of salvation, but were concerning matters of philosophy and such like things.

Objection 4. Moses in Mount Sinai, beside the written law, received from God a more secret doctrine, which he never wrote, but delivered by tradition or word of mouth to the prophets after him. And this the Jews have now set down in their Cabala. *Answer.* This indeed is the opinion of some of the Jews, whom in effect and substance sundry papists follow. But we take it for no better than a Jewish dotage. For if Moses had known any secret doctrine beside the written law, he would never have given this commandment of the said law, "thou shalt not add anything thereto" (Deut. 12:32).

Objection 5. God's Word is of two sorts, "milk" and "strong meat" (Heb. 5:12). By milk we must understand the Word of God written, wherein God speaks plainly to the capacity of the rudest. But strong meat is unwritten traditions, a doctrine not to be delivered unto all but to those that grow to perfection. *Answer.* We must know that one and the same Word of God is milk and strong meat in regard of the manner of handling and propounding of it. For being delivered generally and plainly to the capacity of the simplest, it is milk; but being handled particularly and largely and so fitted for men of more understanding, it is strong meat. As for example, the doctrine of the creation, of man's fall, and redemption by Christ, when it is taught overly and plainly, it is milk. But when the depth of the same is thoroughly opened, it is strong meat. And therefore, it is a conceit of man's brain to imagine that some unwritten word is meant by strong meat.

Objection 6. Sundry places of Scripture be doubtful, and every religion has his several exposition[s] of them, as the papists have theirs, and the Protestants their[s]. Now then seeing there can be but one truth, when [a] question is of the interpretation of Scripture, recourse must be had to the tradition of the church—that the true sense may be determined and the question ended. *Answer.* It is not so.[4] But in doubtful places Scripture itself is sufficient to declare its own meaning; first by the analogy of faith, which is the sum of religion gathered out of the clearest places of Scripture; second, by the circumstances of the place, and the nature and signification of the words; third, by conference of place with place. By these and like helps contained in Scripture, we may judge which is the truest meaning of any place. Scripture itself is the text and the best gloss. And the Scripture is falsely termed the matter of strife, it being not so of itself, but by the abuse of man.

And thus much of our dissent concerning traditions, wherein we must not be wavering but steadfast; because notwithstanding our renouncing of popery, yet popish inclinations and dispositions be rife among us. Our common people marvelously affect human traditions. Yes, man's nature is inclined more to be pleased with them than with the Word of God. The feast of the nativity of our Savior Christ is only a custom and tradition of the church and yet men are commonly more careful to keep it than the Lord's Day—the keeping whereof stands by the moral law. Positive laws are not sufficient to restrain us from buying and selling on the Sabbath, yet within the twelve days no man keeps market. Again, see the truth of this in our affection to the ministry of the Word. Let the preacher allege Peter and Paul, the people count it but common stuff such as any man can bring. But let men come and allege Ambrose, Augustine, and the rest of the fathers—oh, he is the man, he is alone for them. Again, let any man be in danger any way, and straight he sends to the wise man or wizard. God's Word is not sufficient to comfort and direct him. All this argues, that popery denied with the mouth abides still in the heart, and therefore we must learn to reverence the written Word by ascribing unto it all manner of perfection.

4. In the margin: *Aug. de doct. Christ. l.* 1 & 2.

THE EIGHTH POINT

Of Vows

I. Our Consent

Touching vows, this must be known, that we do not condemn them altogether, but only labor to restore the purity of doctrine touching this point, which by the Church of Rome from time to time has been corrupted and defaced. We hold, therefore, that a vow is a promise made to God touching some duties to be performed unto Him and it is twofold: general or special.[1]

The general vow is that which concerns all believers, and it is made in the covenant both of the law and of the gospel. I will here only speak of the vow which is made in the covenant of the gospel, in which there be two actions: one of God, the other of man. God in mercy, on His part, promises to men the remission of sins and life everlasting; and man again, for his part, promises to believe in Christ and to obey God in all His commandments. All men ever made this vow unto God, as the Jews in circumcision, which also they renewed so often as they received the Passover. And in the New Testament, all that are baptized do the

1. This paragraph break is not in the original.

like. And in baptism this vow is called the *stipulation of a good conscience*, whereby we purpose to renounce ourselves, to believe in Christ, and to bring forth the fruits of true repentance. And it ought to be renewed so oft as we are partakers of the Supper of the Lord. This vow is necessary—and must be kept as a part of the true worship of God—because it is a promise wherein we vow to perform all duties commanded of God either in the law or in the gospel. It may be demanded, considering we are bound to obedience, how we bind ourselves in baptism thereto. *Answer.* Though we be already bound, partly by nature, and partly by the written Word, yet may we renew the same bond in a vow. And he that is bound may further bind himself so it be for this end, to help his dullness for want of zeal and to make himself more forward in duties of love to men and the worship of God. To this end, David swore to keep the law of God [Ps. 119:116] though he were bound unto it by nature and by the written law itself.

The special vow is that which does not reach to the person of all believers, but only concerns some special men upon some special occasions. And this kind of vow is twofold:[2]

The first is the vow of a ceremonial duty in the way of service to God, and it was in practice in the church of the Jews under the Old Testament. Examples hereof are two especially. The first was the vow of the Nazarites, whereto no kind of men were bound by God's commandment, but they bound themselves, God only prescribing the manner and order of keeping the same with rites pertaining thereto—as abstinence from wine, the not cutting of their hair, and such like. The second example is of the Jews, when of their own accords they vowed to give God house or land, sheep, or oxen, or any like things, for the maintenance

2. This paragraph break is not in the original.

of the legal worship; and of this also God prescribes certain rules [Leviticus 27]. Now these vows were part of the Jewish pedagogue or ceremonial law, wherein God trained up the Jews in the Old Testament. And being observed of them, they were parts of God's worship. But now under the gospel they are not, being all abolished with the ceremonial law to which Christ put an end at His death upon the cross. It is true, Paul made a vow and since kept the same in the time of the New Testament [Acts 18]—yet not as a part of God's worship, but as a thing indifferent for the time, wherein he only condescended to the weakness of the Jews—that by this means he might bring them the better unto Christ. And whereas Christ is called a Nazarite [Matt. 2:23], we may not think He was of that very order, because He did not abstain from wine. But He was so termed because He was the verity and accomplishment of this order. For by it was signified that God's church was a peculiar people, severed or chosen out of the world, and that Christ—in respect of holiness—was also separated from all sinners. And the words in Saint Matthew, "He shall be called a Nazarite," are borrowed from the book of Judges, chapter 13, where they are properly spoken of Samson, and in type or figure of Christ. For as Samson saved Israel by his death, so did Christ save His church. And as Samson killed his enemies more by death than by life, so did Christ. It is plain therefore, that this kind of vow binds us not. For there are no more ceremonies to be kept under the gospel for parts of God's worship, but the outward rites of baptism and the Lord's Supper. Vows concerning meats, drinks, attire, touching, tasting, times, places, [and] days, were proper to the Jews.

The second kind of special vow is that whereby a man promises freely to perform some outward and bodily exercise for some good end. And this vow also (if it be made accordingly) is lawful and belongs both to the church of the Old and New

Testaments. In the Old we have the example of the Rechabites [Jer. 35:6], who by the appointment of Jonadab their father, abstained from strong drink and wine, from planting vineyards and orchards—whereby Jonadab intended only to break them beforehand and to acquaint them with their future condition and state, that they should be strangers in a foreign land; that so they might prepare themselves to endure hardness in the time to come. And now in the New Testament we have warrant in like manner to vow—as if a man, by drinking of wine or strong drink find himself prone to drunkenness, he may vow with himself to drink no more wine nor strong drink for so long time as he feels the drinking thereof will stir up his infirmity and minister occasion of sinning. Of this kind also are the vows in which we purpose and promise to God to keep set times of fasting, to task ourselves in prayer and reading of Holy Scriptures, and to give set alms for special causes known to ourselves, and to do sundry like duties. And that we be not deceived in making such vows, certain rules must be remembered: 1. That the vow be agreeable to God's will and Word, for if it be otherwise, the making—as also the keeping thereof—is sin. Vows must not be the bonds of iniquity. 2. It must so be made that it may stand with Christian liberty. For we may not make such things necessary in conscience which God has made free. Now Christian liberty allows unto us the free use of all things indifferent, so it be out of the case of offence. Hence it follows that vows must be made and kept, or not kept, so far forth as in conscience they may stand, or not stand, with our liberty purchased by Christ.

The vow must be made with consent of superiors, if we be under government. Thus, among the Jews, the vow of a daughter might not stand, unless the consent of parents came thereunto. 4. It must be in the power and ability of the maker thereof to do or not to do. A vow made of a thing impossible is no vow. 5. It must be agreeable to the calling of him that makes it, that is, both to his general calling as he is a Christian and to that particular calling wherein he lives. If it be against either one or both, it is unlawful. 6. It must be made with deliberation. Rash vows be not lawful, though the things vowed may be done lawfully. 7. The end must be good, which is, to preserve and exercise the gifts of faith, prayer, repentance, obedience, and other virtues of the mind; also to testify our thankfulness unto God for blessings received. These are the principal rules which must be observed in making of vows; and herewithal must be remembered that vows made on this manner are by themselves no part of God's worship, but only helps and furtherances thereunto—and thus we are to esteem of all the vows of the New Testament. And thus much of special vows and of our consent herein.

II. The Dissent or Difference

The points of difference between us touching vows are especially three:[3]

Point of difference 1. The Church of Rome teaches that in the New Testament we are as much bound to make vows as was the church of the Jews and that even in external exercises. We say no, considering the ceremonial law is now abolished, and we have only two ceremonies by commandment to be observed: baptism, and the Supper of the Lord. Again, we are not so much bound to make or keep vows as the Jews were, because they had a commandment so to do and we have none at all. But they allege to the contrary the prophet Isaiah, who speaking of the time of the gospel says, "The Egyptians shall know the Lord, and shall vow unto Him and keep it" (Isa. 19:21). I answer two ways: first, that the prophet in this place expresses and signifies the spiritual worship of the New Testament by ceremonial worship then used, as he does

3. This paragraph break is not in the original.

also in the last chapter where he calls the ministers of the New Testament *priests* and *Levites*. Second, we grant, the church of the New Testament makes vows unto God, but they are of moral and evangelical duties which must not be left undone—and if vowing will indeed further them, it is not to be neglected. And therefore, so often as we come to the Lord's Table, we in heart renew the vow and promise of obedience. And though vows be made of things and actions indifferent, yet are they not any parts of God's worship, which is the point to be proved.

Again, they allege, "Vow unto God and perform it" (Ps. 76:11). And they say that this commandment binds all men. *Answer*. That commandment first binds the Jews to the making of ceremonial vows. Again, David here speaks of the vowing of praise and thanksgiving unto God, and so he expounds himself, "My vows are upon me, I will offer praises unto God" (Ps. 56:12). And this vow indeed concerns all men because it respects a moral duty, which is to set forth the praise of God.

Point of difference 2. They also hold that vows made even of things not commanded—as meats, drinks, attire, etc.—are parts of God's worship, yes, that they tend to a state of perfection in that the keeping of them brings man to a higher estate than the keeping of the law can do. We flatly say no, holding that lawful vows be certain stays and props of God's worship and not the worship itself.[4] For Paul says plainly, "Bodily exercise profiteth little, but godliness is profitable for much" (1 Tim. 4:8). Again, as God's kingdom is, so must His worship be—and God's kingdom stands not in outward things, as in eating, drinking, and such like actions—and therefore His worship stands not in outward things.

Point of difference 3. They maintain such vows to be made as are not agreeable to the rules before named. And herein also we

4. In the margin: *Adminicula cultus divina*.

are to dissent from them. The first and principal is the vow of continence, whereby a man promises to God to keep chastity always in single life, that is, out of the estate of wedlock. This kind of vow is flat against the Word of God, and therefore unlawful. For Paul says, "If they cannot contain, let them marry" (1 Cor. 7:9). It is "a doctrine of devils" (1 Tim. 4:1) to forbid to marry. "Marriage is honorable among all, and the bed undefiled" (Heb. 13:4). Again, this vow is not in the power of himself that vows, for continence is the gift of God, who gives it not unto all, but to whom He will, and when He will, and as long as He will. They allege that in the want of continence, fasting and prayer obtain it. *Answer.* It is not so. God's gifts be of two sorts: some are common to all believers, as the gift of faith, repentance, and the fear of God, etc. Others are peculiar to some only, as the gift of continence. "I would that all men were as I myself am, but every man has his proper gift of God, one this way, another that way" (1 Cor. 7:7). Now if we fast and pray for the increase of the common gifts of God, as faith, repentance, and all such as are needful to salvation, we may obtain them in some measure, but the like cannot be said of particular gifts. The child of God may pray for health or wealth and not obtain either of them in this world; because it is not the will of God to vouchsafe these blessings to all men. And Paul prayed three times to be delivered from a temptation, and yet obtained not his suit. And so may we likewise pray for chastity in single estate, and yet never obtain it; because, it may be, it is the will of God to save us without it. This vow therefore we abhor as a thing that has heretofore—and does still—bring forth innumerable abominations in[to] the world. Yet here mark in what manner we do it. First of all, though we dislike the vow, yet we like and commend single life. Marriage indeed is better in two respects: first, because God has ordained it to be a remedy of continence to all such persons as cannot contain; second, because it is the seminary both of church and commonwealth; and it brings forth a *seed of God* for the enlarging of His kingdom [Mal. 2:15]. Yet single life in them that have the gift of continence is in some respects to be preferred. First, because it brings liberty in persecution. Thus, Paul says, "I suppose it to be good for the present necessity for a man so to be" (1 Cor. 7:26). Second, because it frees men from the common cares, molestations, and distractions that be in the family. "Such shall have trouble in the flesh, but I spare you" (v. 28). Third, because single parties do commonly with more bodily ease and liberty worship God, it being still presupposed that they have the gift of continence. "The unmarried woman careth for the things of the Lord, that she may be holy both in body and spirit" (v. 34).

Again, though we dislike the vow, yet we hold and teach that men or women being assured that they have the gift of continence, may constantly resolve and purpose with themselves to live and lead a single life. "He that standeth firm in his own heart, that hath no need, but hath power of his own will, and hath so decreed *in his heart* that he will keep his virgin, he doth well" (1 Cor. 7:37). And we embrace the saying of Theodoret on 1 Timothy 4: "For he does not," says he, "blame single life or continence, but he accuses them that *by law enacted compel* men to follow these." And men made themselves chaste for the kingdom of heaven [Matt. 19:12], not by vow, but by a purpose of heart, which is far less than a vow, and may be changed upon occasion, whereas a vow cannot, unless it evidently appears to be unlawful.

Third, for such persons as are able to contain—to live single for the ends before named—indeed we hold it to be no counsel of perfection, yet do we not deny it to be a counsel of expedience or outward ease according to that which Paul says, "I give mine advice..." (v. 25), and, "I speak this for your commodity, not to entangle you in a snare" (v. 35).

Lastly, we think, that if any having the gift of continence do make a vow to live single and yet afterward marry (the said gift remaining), they have sinned. Yet not because they are married, but because their vow is broken. And thus said Augustine of widows that married after their vow: *lib. de bono viduit. cap.* 9.

The second is the vow of poverty and monastic life in which men bestow all they have on the poor and give themselves wholly and only to prayer and fasting. This vow is against the will of God. "It is a more blessed thing to give than to receive" (Acts 20:35). "Give me neither riches nor poverty" (Prov. 30:8). Poverty is numbered among the curses of the law [Deut. 28:22], none whereof are to be vowed. And it is the rule of the Holy Ghost, "He that will not labor," namely in some special and warrantable calling, "must not eat" (2 Thess. 3:10). And, "I exhort that they work with quietness, and eat their own bread" (v. 12). Now when as men live apart from others, giving themselves only to prayer and fasting, they live in no calling. And it is against the general vow made in baptism, because it frees men from sundry duties of the moral law and changes the proper end of man's life. For every man must have two callings. The first is the general calling of a Christian by virtue of which he performs worship unto God and duties of love to men. The second is a particular calling, wherein according to his gift, he must do service to men in some function, pertaining either to the church or commonwealth whereof he is a member. And the first of these two must be performed in the second, and the second in and with the first. The end of man's life is not only to serve God by the duties of the first table, but by serving of man in the duties of the second table, to serve God. And therefore, the love of our neighbor is called the "fulfilling of the whole law" (Rom. 13:10), because the law of God is practiced not apart, but in and with the love of our neighbor. This being so, it is manifest that vowed poverty in monkish life makes many unprofitable members both of church and commonwealth.

And though we dislike this vow also, yet we do it holding these conclusions:[5]

Conclusion 1. That a man may forsake all his goods upon special calling, as the apostles did when they were sent to preach the gospel through the whole world. Second, goods may be forsaken, yes wife, children, parents, brethren, and all, in the case of confession, that is, when a man for the religion of Christ is persecuted and constrained to forsake all he has. For then the second table gives place to the duties of the first [Mark 10:29].[6]

Conclusion 2. That for the time of persecution men may withdraw themselves (just occasion offered) and go apart to wildernesses or like places [Heb. 11:38], yet for the time of peace, I see no cause of solitary life. If it be alleged that men go apart for contemplation and spiritual exercises, I say again, that God's graces may as well be exercised in the family as in the cloister. The family is indeed as it were a school of God, in which they that have but a spark of grace may learn and exercise many virtues: the acknowledgment of God, invocation, the fear of God, love, bountifulness, patience, meekness, faithfulness, etc. No, here be more occasions of doing or taking good than be or can be in a cloister.[7]

Conclusion 3. That we condemn not the old and ancient monks, though we like not everything in them.[8] For they lived not like idle-bellies, but in the sweat of their own brows, as they ought to do. And many of them were married, and in their meat, drink, apparel, rule, vow, and whole course of life differed from the monks of this time; even as far as heaven [is] from earth.[9]

---

5. This paragraph break is not in the original.

6. This paragraph break is not in the original.

7. This paragraph break is not in the original.

8. In the margin: *Zozom. l.* 1. *c.* 13.

9. In the margin: *Epiph. haer.* 78. *August. de Mor. Eccl. l.* 2. *c.* 31 & *de oper. Monach. cap.* 17.

The third vow is a regular obedience, whereby men give themselves to keep some devised rule or order, standing most commonly in the observation of exercises in outward things, as meats, and drinks, and apparel, etc. This vow is against Christian liberty, whereby is granted a free use of all things indifferent, so it be without the case of offence. "Stand fast in the liberty wherein Christ hath made you free" (Gal. 5:1). "Let no man judge you in meat and drink" (Col. 2:16).[10]

To conclude, whereas the papists magnify these their vows, and yet make no such account of the vow in baptism, we for our parts must be contrary to them, not only in judgment, but also in practice. And we ought to have special care to make good the vows we have plight[11] to God according to His commandment. In our creation we made a vow of obedience. And being received into the covenant of grace, we vowed to believe in Christ, and to bring forth fruits of new obedience, and this vow is renewed as oft as we come to the Lord's Table. Our duty therefore is to perform them also to God, as David says, "Vow unto God and keep it" (Ps. 76:11). And if we keep them not, all turns to our shame and confusion. Men stand much on the keeping of that word which they have passed to men, and it is taken for a point of much honesty, as it is indeed. Now then, if there be such care to keep covenant with men, much more should we have care to keep covenant with God.

---

10. This paragraph break is not in the original.

11. *Plight*: pledged.

THE NINTH POINT

Of Images

I. Our Consent

Conclusion 1. We acknowledge the civil use of images as freely and truly as the Church of Rome does. By *civil use* I understand that use which is made of them in the common societies of men, out of the appointed places of the solemn worship of God. And this to be lawful, it appears, because the arts of painting and engraving are the ordinance of God, and to be skillful in them is the gift of God, as the example of Bezaleel and Aholiab declare [Ex. 35:30, 34]. This use of images may be in sundry things: 1. In the adorning and setting forth of buildings; thus Solomon beautified his throne with the images of lions. And the Lord commanded His temple to be adorned with the images of palm trees, of pomegranates, of bulls, cherubs, and such like. 2. It serves for the distinction of coins, according to the practice of emperors and princes of all nations. When Christ was asked [in] Matthew 22 whether it was lawful to give tribute to Caesar or no, He called for a penny and said, "Whose image or superscription is this?" They said, "Caesar's." He then said, "Give to Caesar the things that are Caesar's," not condemning but approving the stamp or image upon his coin. And though the Jews were forbidden to make images in way of representation, or worship of the true God, yet the cycle of the sanctuary, which they used, especially after the time of Moses, was stamped with the image of the almond tree and the pot of manna. 3. Images serve to keep in memory friends deceased, whom we reverence. And it is like that hence came one occasion of the images that are now in use in the Roman Church. For in the days of the apostles, men used privately to keep the pictures of their friends departed. And this practice after crept into the open congregation; and at the last, superstition getting head, images began to be worshipped.

Conclusion 2. We hold the historical use of images to be good and lawful—and that is to represent to the eye the acts of histories, whether they be human or divine. And thus we think the histories of the Bible may be painted in private places.

Conclusion 3. In one case it is lawful to make an image to testify the presence or the effects of the majesty of God, namely, when God Himself gives any special commandment so to do. In this case Moses made and erected a brazen serpent to be a type, sign, or image to represent Christ crucified [John 3:14]. And the cherubs over the mercy seat served to represent the majesty of God, to whom the angels are subject [Ex. 25:18]. And in the second commandment it is not simply said, "Thou shalt not make a graven image," but with limitation, "Thou shalt not make *to thyself*," that is, on your own head, upon your own will and pleasure.

Conclusion 4. The right images of the New Testament, which we hold and acknowledge, are the doctrine and preaching of the gospel, and all things that by the Word of God pertain thereto. "Who hath bewitched you that ye should not obey the truth, to whom Jesus Christ was before described in your sight, and among you crucified?" (Gal. 3:1). Hence it follows that the preaching of the Word is as a most excellent picture in which Christ with His benefits are lively represented unto us. And we dissent not from Origen, contra *Cels. lib.* 8, who says, "We have no images framed by any base workmen, but such as are brought forth and framed by the Word of God, namely, patterns of virtue, and frames resembling Christians." He means that Christians themselves are the images of Christians.

II. The Difference

Our dissent from them touching images stands in three points:

Difference 1. The Church of Rome holds it lawful for them to make images to resemble God, though not in respect of His divine nature; yet in respect of some properties and actions. We on the contrary hold it unlawful for us to make any image, any way to represent the true God, or to make an image of anything in way of religion to worship God, much less the creature thereby. For the second commandment says plainly, "Thou shalt not make to thyself any graven image, or the likeness of anything in heaven, etc." (Ex. 20:4). The papists say the commandment is meant of the images of false gods. But, will they, nill they, it must be understood of the images of the true Jehovah. And it forbids us[1] to resemble God either in His nature, properties, or works, or to use any resemblance of Him for any sacred use—as to help the memory when we are about to worship God. Thus much the Holy Ghost, who is the best expounder of Himself, teaches most plainly. "Thou sawest no image at all (either of false or true God) and therefore thou shalt not make any likeness of anything" (Deut. 4:15–16). And again, the prophet Isaiah, reproving idolaters, asks, "to whom they will liken God, or what similitude will they set up unto Him?" (Isa. 40:18). And, "Know

1. In the margin: So says Roman Catech. on 2nd Command.

ye nothing? Have ye not heard? Hath it not been told you *from the beginning*?" (v. 21). As if he should say, "Have you forgotten the second commandment that God gave unto your fathers?" And thus, he flatly reproves all them that resemble the true God in images. But they say further that by "images" in the second commandment are meant "idols," that is (say they) such things as men worship for gods. *Answer.* If it were so, we should confound the first and second commandments. For the first, "Thou shalt have no other gods before my face," forbids all false gods which man wickedly frames unto himself, by giving his heart and the principal affections thereof to them. And therefore, idols also are here forbidden when they are esteemed as gods. And the distinction they make that an image is the representation of true things, and idol of things supposed, is false. Tertullian says, that every *form* or representation is to be termed an *idol.*[2] And Isidore says that the heathen used the names of *image* and *idol* indifferently in one and the same signification.[3] And Saint Stephen in his apology calls the golden calf an *idol* [Acts 7:41]. Jerome says that idols are images of dead men.[4] Ancient divines accord with all this which I have said. Lactantius says, *Inst. lib.* 2. *cap.* 19, "Where images are for religion's sake, there is no religion." The Council of Elibera, *can.* 36, decreed, that "nothing should be painted on the walls of churches, which is adored of the people." Origen, "We suffer not any to worship Jesus at altars, images, and temples, *because it is written*, 'Thou shalt have none other gods.'"[5] And Epiphanius says, "It is against the authority of the Scriptures to see the image of Christ or of any saints hanging in the church."[6] In the seventh

2. In the margin: *De Idol. c.* 3.
3. In the margin: *Etym. l.* 8.
4. In the margin: *In Isay.* 37.
5. In the margin: *Contr. Cels. lib.* 7.
6. In the margin: *Epist. ad Ioh. Hierus.*

Council of Constantinople these words of Epiphanius are cited against the Encratitae: "Be mindful, beloved children, not to bring images into the church, nor set them in the places where the saints are buried, *but always carry God in your hearts*. Neither let them be suffered in any common house: for it is not meet that a Christian should be occupied by the eyes, but by the meditation of the mind."

Arguments of the Papists

The reasons which they use to defend their opinions are these:[7]

Objection 1. In Solomon's temple were erected cherubims, which were images of angels on the mercy seat where God was worshipped [1 Kings 6:27], and thereby was resembled the majesty of God. Therefore, it is lawful to make images to resemble God. *Answer.* They were erected by special commandment from God, who prescribed the very form of them and the place where they must be set. And thereby Moses had a warrant to make them, otherwise he had sinned. Let them show the like warrant for their images if they can. Second, the cherubims were placed in the Holy of Holies, in the most inward place of the temple, and consequently were removed from the sight of the people, who only heard of them. And none but the high priest saw them, and that but once a year. And the cherubims without the veil, though they were to be seen, yet were they not to be worshipped [Ex. 20:4]. Therefore, they serve nothing at all to justify the images of the Church of Rome.

Objection 2. God appeared in the form of a man to Abraham [Gen. 18:1–13], and to Daniel, who saw the Ancient of Days sitting on a throne [Dan. 7:9]. Now as God appeared, so may He be resembled. "Therefore," say they, "it is lawful to resemble God in

7. This paragraph break is not in the original.

the form of a man or any like image in which He showed Himself to men." *Answer.* In this reason the proposition is false, for God may appear in whatsoever form it pleases His majesty; yet it does not follow, that man should therefore resemble God in those forms—man having no liberty to resemble Him in any form at all unless he be commanded so to do. Again, when God appeared in the form of a man, that form was a sign of God's presence only for the time when God appeared and no longer—as the bread and wine in the sacrament are signs of Christ's body and blood, not forever, but for the time of administration, for afterward they become again as common bread and wine. And when the Holy Ghost appeared in the likeness of a dove, that likeness was a sign of His presence no longer than the Holy Ghost so appeared. And therefore, he that would in these forms represent the Trinity, greatly dishonors God and does that for which he has no warrant.

Objection 3. Man is the image of God, but it is lawful to paint a man and therefore to make the image of God. *Answer.* A very cavil. For first, a man cannot be painted, as he is the image of God which stands in the spiritual gifts of righteousness and true holiness. Again, the image of a man may be painted for civil or historical use, but to paint any man for this end to represent God, or in the way of religion, that we may the better remember and worship God, it is unlawful. Other reasons which they use are of small moment, and therefore I omit them.

Difference 2. They teach and maintain that images of God and of saints may be worshipped with religious worship, especially the crucifix. For Thomas of Watering says, "Seeing the cross represents Christ, who died upon a cross and is to be worshipped with divine honor, it follows that the cross is to be worshipped so too."[8]

8. In the margin: *Summ. part* 3. *quest.* 35. *art.* 3.

We on the contrary hold they may not. Our principal ground is the second commandment, which contains two parts: the first forbids the making of images to resemble the true God; the second forbids the worshipping of them, or God in them in these words, "Thou shalt not bow down to them" (Ex. 20:5). Now, there can be no worship done to anything less than the bending of the knee. Again, the brazen serpent was a type or image of Christ crucified [John 3:14], appointed by God Himself. Yet when the people burned incense to it [2 Kings 18:4], Hezekiah broke it in pieces and is therefore commended. And when the devil bade our Savior Christ but to bow down the knee unto him and he would give Him the whole world, Christ rejects his offer, saying, "Thou shalt worship the Lord thy God, and him only shalt thou serve" (Matt. 4:10). Again, it is lawful for one man to worship another with civil worship, but to worship man with religious honor is unlawful. For all religious worship is prescribed in the first table, and the honor due to man is only prescribed in the second table. And the first commandment thereof, "Honor thy father..." (Ex. 20:12), which honor is therefore civil and not religious. Now the meanest man that can be is a more excellent image of God than all the images of God or of saints that are devised by men. Augustine, and long after him Gregory, in plain terms deny images to be adored.[9]

The papists defend their opinions by these reasons:[10]

Objection 1. "Cast down yourselves before his footstool" (Ps. 99:5). *Answer.* The words are thus to be read: "Bow at his footstool," that is, at the ark and mercy seat; for there He has made a promise of His presence. The words therefore say not, "bow to the ark," but to God at the ark.

---

9. In the margin: *De morib. eccles. cap.* 35. *lib.* 9. *epast.* 9.

10. This paragraph break is not in the original.

Objection 2. God said to Moses, "Stand afar off and put off thy shoes, for the place is holy" (Ex. 3:5). Now if holy places must be reverenced, then much more holy images, as the cross of Christ and such like. *Answer.* God commanded the ceremony of putting off the shoes that He might thereby strike Moses with a religious reverence—not of the place, but of His own majesty—whose presence made the place holy. Let them show the like warrant for images.

Objection 3. It is lawful to kneel down to a chair of estate in the absence of the king or queen, therefore much more to the images of God and of saints in heaven glorified, being absent from us. *Answer.* To kneel to the chair of estate is no more but a civil testimony, or sign of civil reverence, by which all good subjects when occasion is offered show their loyalty and subjection to their lawful princes. And this kneeling being on this manner, and to no other end, has sufficient warrant in the Word of God. But kneeling to the image of any saint departed is religious—and consequently more than civil—worship, as the papists themselves confess. The argument then proves nothing, unless they will keep themselves to one and the same kind of worship.

Difference 3.[11] The papists also teach that God may be lawfully worshipped in images in which He has appeared unto men—as the Father, in the image of an old man; the Son, in the image of a man crucified; and the Holy Ghost, in the likeness of a dove, etc. But we hold it unlawful to worship God in, by, or at any image. For this is the thing which (as I have proved before) the second commandment forbids. And the act of the Israelites [Exodus 32] in worshipping the golden calf is condemned as flat idolatry, albeit they worshipped not the calf, but God in the calf. For Aaron

11. This paragraph is mislabelled "Difference 2" in the 1635 edition.

says, "Tomorrow shall be the solemnity of Jehovah" (v. 5), whereby he gives us to understand that the calf was but a sign of Jehovah whom they worshipped. *Objection.* It seems the Israelites worshipped the calf, for Aaron says, "These be thy gods (O Israel) that brought thee out of Egypt" (v. 4). *Answer.* Aaron's meaning is nothing else, but that the golden calf was a sign of the presence of the true God. And the name of the thing signified is given to the sign, as upon a stage he is called a king that represents the king. And Augustine says that "images are wont to be called by the names of things whereof they are images, *as the counterfeit of* Samuel *is called* Samuel."[12] And we must not esteem them all as mad men to think that a calf made of their earrings, being but one or two days old, should be the God that brought them out of Egypt with a mighty hand many days before.

And these are the points of difference touching images wherein we must stand at variance forever with the Church of Rome. For they err in the foundation of religion, making indeed an idol of the true God, and worshipping another Christ than we do—under new terms maintaining the idolatry of the heathen. And therefore have we departed from them—and so must we still do—because they are idolaters, as I have proved.

12. In the margin: *Ad Simplic. lib.* 2. *q*. 3.

THE TENTH POINT

Of Real Presence

I. Our Consent

We hold and believe a presence of Christ's body and blood in the sacrament of the Lord's Supper, and that not feigned, but a true and real presence, which must be considered two ways: first, in respect of the signs; second, in respect of the communicants. For the first, we hold and teach that Christ's body and blood are truly present with the bread and wine, being signs in the sacrament. But how? Not in respect of place, of coexistence, but by sacramental relation, on this manner: When a word is uttered, the sound comes to the ear; and at the same instant, the thing signified comes to the mind; and thus, by relation, the word and the thing spoken of are both present together. Even so at the Lord's Table, bread and wine must not be considered barely as substances and creatures, but as outward signs in relation to the body and blood of Christ. And this relation, arising from the very institution of the Sacrament, stands in this, that when the elements of bread and wine are present to the hand and to the mouth of the receiver, at the very same time the body and blood of Christ are presented to the mind. Thus and no otherwise is Christ truly present with the signs. The second presence is in respect of the communicants, to whose believing hearts He is also really present. It will be said, what kind of presence is this? *Answer.* Such as the communion in the sacrament is, such is the presence—and by the communion must we judge of the presence. Now the communion is on this manner: God the Father, according to the tenor of the evangelical covenant, gives Christ in His sacrament as really and truly as anything can be given unto man—not by part and piecemeal (as we say)—but whole Christ, God and man, on this sort. In Christ there be two natures, the Godhead, and manhood. The Godhead is not given in regard of substance or essence, but only in regard of efficacy, merits,[1] and operation conveyed thence to the manhood.[2]

And further, in this sacrament, Christ's whole manhood is given, both body and soul, in this order: First of all is given the very manhood in respect of substance, and that really; second the merits and benefits thereof, as namely the satisfaction performed by and in the manhood to the justice of God. And thus the entire manhood—with the benefits thereof—are given wholly and jointly together. For the two distinct signs of bread and wine signify not two distinct givings of the body apart and the blood apart, but the full and perfect nourishment of our souls. Again, the benefits of Christ's manhood are diversely given, some by imputation, which is an action of God accepting that which is done by Christ as done by us. And thus it has pleased God to give the passion of Christ and His obedience. Some again are given by a kind of propagation, which I cannot fitly express in terms, but I resemble it thus. As one candle is lighted by another, and one torch or candlelight is conveyed to twenty candles, even so the inherent righteousness of every believer is derived from the storehouse of righteousness,

1. In the margin: *Ad Simplic. lib.* 2. *q.* 3.

2. This paragraph break is not the original.

which is in the manhood of Christ. For the righteousness of all the members is but the fruit thereof, even as the natural corruption in all mankind is but a fruit of that original sin which was in Adam. Thus we see how God, for His part, gives Christ, and that really. To proceed, when God gives Christ, He gives withal at the same time the Spirit of Christ, which Spirit creates in the heart of the receiver the instrument of true faith, by which the heart really receives Christ given of God by resting upon the promise which God has made, that He will give Christ and His righteousness to every true believer. Now then, when God gives Christ with His benefits, and man for his part by faith receives the same as they are given, there rises that union which is between every good receiver and Christ Himself. Which union is not forged, but a real, true, and near conjunction; nearer than which, none is or can be—because it is made by a solemn giving and receiving that passes between God and man, as also by the bond of one and the same Spirit. To come then to the point, considering there is a real union, and consequently a real communion between us and Christ (as I have proved), there must needs be such a kind of presence wherein Christ is truly and really present to the heart of him that receives the sacrament in faith. And thus far do we consent with the Romish Church touching real presence.

II. The Dissent

We differ not touching the presence itself, but only in the manner of presence. For though we hold a real presence of Christ's body and blood in the sacrament, yet do we not take it to be local, bodily, or substantial, but spiritual and mystical; to the signs by sacramental relation, and to the communicants by faith alone. On the contrary, the Church of Rome maintains transubstantiation, that is, a local, bodily, and substantial presence of Christ's body and blood, by a change and conversion of the bread and wine into the said body and blood.

Our Reasons

Reason 1. This corporal presence overturns sundry articles of faith. For we believe that the body of Christ was made of the pure substance of the virgin Mary and that but once, namely, when He was conceived by the Holy Ghost and born. But this cannot stand if the body of Christ be made of bread and His blood of wine, as they must needs be if there be no succession or annihilation but a real conversion of substances in the sacrament—unless we must believe contrarieties, that His body was made of the substance of the virgin and not of the virgin; made once, and not once but often. Again, if His body and blood be under the forms of bread and wine, then is He not as yet ascended into heaven but remains still among us. Neither can He be said to come from heaven at the Day of Judgment, for He that must come thence to judge the quick and dead must be absent from the earth. And this was the ancient faith. Augustine says that "Christ according to His majesty and providence and grace is present with us to the end of the world, but according to His *assumed flesh He is not* always with us."[3] Cyril says, "He is *absent in body*, and present in virtue, whereby all things are governed."[4] Vigilius says, that "He is *gone* from us *according to His humanity.* He has left us in His humanity, in the form of a servant absent from us. When His flesh was on earth, He was not in heaven. Being on earth, He was not in heaven. And being now in heaven, He is not on earth."[5] Fulgentius says, "One and the same Christ, according to His human

---

3. In the margin: *Tract.* 1 *in Joh.*

4. In the margin: *Lib.* 9 *in Joh. c.* 21.

5. In the margin: *Cont. Eutych. l.* 1 & 4.

substance, was absent from heaven when He was on earth, and *left the earth* when He ascended into heaven."[6]

Reason 2. The bodily presence overturns the nature of a true body, whose common nature or essential property it is to have length, breadth, and thickness; which being taken away, a body is no more a body. And by reason of these three dimensions, a body can occupy but one place at once; as Aristotle said, the property of a body is to be seated in some place, so as a man may say where it is.[7] They therefore that hold the body of Christ to be in many places at once, do make it no body at all, but rather a spirit and that infinite. They allege that God is almighty—that is true indeed—but in this and like matters we must not dispute what God can do but what He will do. And I say further, because God is omnipotent, therefore there be some things which He cannot do, as for Him to deny Himself, to lie, and to make the parts of a contradiction to be both true at the same time. To come to the point, if God should make the very body of Christ to be in many places at once, He should make it to be no body while it remains a body; and to be circumscribed in some one place and not circumscribed, because it is in many places at the same time; to be visible in heaven and invisible in the sacrament. And thus should He make contradictions to be true, which to do is against His nature and argues rather impotency than power. Augustine says to this purpose, "If He could lie, deceive, be deceived, steal unjustly, He should not be omnipotent." And, "Therefore He is omnipotent, because He *cannot do* these things." Again, "He is called omnipotent by doing that which He will, and not by doing that which He will not, which, if it should befall Him, He should not be omnipotent."[8]

---

6. In the margin: *Lib.* 2. *ad Thrasimundum.*

7. In the margin: *Cap. de categor. quant.*

8. In the margin: *De Symb. ad Catech. l.* 1 *c.* 1.

Reason 3. Transubstantiation overturns the very Supper of the Lord. For in every sacrament there must be a sign, a thing signified, and a proportion or relation between them both. But popish real presence takes all away. For when the bread is really turned into Christ's body and the wine into His blood, then the sign is abolished, and there remains nothing but the outward forms or appearance of bread and wine. Again, it abolishes the ends of the sacrament whereof one is to remember Christ until His coming again, who being present in the sacrament bodily, needs not to be remembered, because helps of remembrance are of things absent. Another end is to nourish the soul unto eternal life. But by transubstantiation the principal feeding is of the body and not of the soul, which is only fed with spiritual food. For though the body may be bettered by the food of the soul, yet cannot the soul be fed with bodily food.

Reason 4. In the sacrament, the body of Christ is received as it was crucified, and His blood as it was shed upon the cross. But now at this time, Christ's body crucified remains still as a body, but not as a body crucified, because the act of crucifying is ceased. Therefore, it is faith alone that makes Christ crucified to be present unto us in the sacrament. Again, that blood which ran out of the feet and hands and side of Christ upon the cross was not gathered up again and put into veins; no, the collection was needless because after the resurrection He lived no more a natural but a spiritual life. And none knows what is become of this blood. The papist therefore cannot say it is present under the form of wine locally. And we may better say it is received spiritually by faith, whose property is to give a being to things which are not.

Reason 5. The fathers of the Old Testament did eat the same spiritual meat and drink the same spiritual drink, for they drank of the rock, which was Christ [1 Cor. 10:3]. Now they could not eat His body which was crucified or drink

His blood shed bodily, but by faith, because then His body and blood were not in nature. The papists make answer that the fathers did eat the same meat and drink the same spiritual drink with themselves, not with us. But their answer is against the text. For the apostle's intent is to prove that the Jews were every way equal to the Corinthians because they did eat the same spiritual meat and drink the same spiritual drink with the Corinthians. Otherwise, his reason proves not the point which he has in hand, namely, that the Israelites were nothing inferior to the Corinthians.

Reason 6. And it is said, the Sabbath "was made for man, and not man for the Sabbath" (Mark 2:27), so it may be said that the sacrament of the Lord's Supper was made for man, and not man for it, and therefore man is more excellent than the sacrament. But if the signs of bread and wine be really turned into the body and blood of Christ, then is the sacrament infinitely better than man, who in his best estate is only joined to Christ and made a member of His mystical body—whereas the bread and wine are made very Christ. But the sacrament or outward elements indeed are not better than man, the end being always better than the thing ordained to the end. It remains therefore that Christ's presence is not corporal but spiritual. Again, in the Supper of the Lord, every believer receives [the] whole Christ, God and man, though not the Godhead. Now by this carnal eating, we receive not [the] whole Christ, but only a part of His manhood, and therefore in the sacrament there is no carnal eating and consequently no bodily presence.

Reason 7. The judgment of the ancient church. Theodoret says, "The same Christ who called His natural body food and bread, who also called Himself a vine, He vouchsafed the visible signs the name of His own body, *not changing nature,* but putting grace to nature, *whereby He means consecration*."[9] And, "The mystical signs after sanctification lose not their proper nature. For they *remain in their first nature* and keep their first figure and form; and as before, may be touched and seen. And [that] which they are made is understood, believed, and adored."[10] Gelasius says, "Bread and wine pass into the substance of the body and blood of Christ, yet so as the *substance or nature of bread and wine ceases not*. And they are turned into the divine substance, yet the bread and wine *remain still in the property of their nature*."[11] Lombard says, "If it be asked what conversion this is, whether formal or substantial, or of another kind, I am not able to define."[12] And that the fathers held not transubstantiation, I prove it by sundry reasons: First, they used in former times "to burn with fire that" which remained after the administration of the Lord's Supper.[13] Second, by the sacramental union of the bread and wine with the body and blood of Christ, they used to confirm the personal union of the manhood of Christ with the Godhead against heretics—which argument they would not have used if they had believed [in] a popish real presence. Third, it was a custom in Constantinople, that if many parts of the sacrament remained after the administration thereof was ended, "that young children should be sent for from the school to eat them"; who nevertheless were barred [from] the Lord's Table.[14] And this argues plainly that the church in those days took the bread after the administration was ended for common bread. Again, it was once an order in the Roman Church that the wine should be "consecrated by

9. In the margin: *Dialog*. 1. *immutab.*

10. In the margin: Same Dialog.

11. In the margin: *Lib. de duab. Nat. Christ.*

12. In the margin: *Lib*. 4. *dist*. 11.

13. In the margin: *Hesych. l*. 2. *c*. 8 *in Levit. Theodo. dialog.*

14. In the margin: *Evag. l*. 4. *Niceph. i*. 17. *c*. 25.

dipping into it bread, which had been consecrated."[15] But this order cannot stand with the real presence in which the bread is turned both into the body and blood. Nicholaus Cabasilas says, "After he has used some speech to the people, he erects their minds, and lifts their thoughts from earth, and says, *Surfum corda*, 'Let us lift up our hearts, let us *think on things above* and not on things that are upon the earth.' They consent and say that they lift up their hearts thither, where there is treasure, and where Christ sits at the right hand of His Father."[16]

III. Objections of Papists

Objection 1. The first reason is, "My flesh is meat indeed and my blood is drink indeed" (John 6:55). "Therefore," say they, "Christ's body must be eaten with the mouth and His blood drunk accordingly." *Answer.* The chapter must be understood of a spiritual eating of Christ. His body is meat indeed, but spiritual meat, and His blood spiritual drink, to be received not by the mouth but by faith. This is the very point that Christ here intends to prove, namely, that to believe in Him, to eat His flesh and to drink His blood, are all one. Again, this chapter must not be understood of that special eating of Christ in the sacrament. For it is said generally, "Except ye eat the flesh of Christ and drink his blood, ye have no life in you" (v. 53). And if these very words (which are the substance of the chapter) must be understood of a sacramental eating, no man before the coming of Christ was saved. For none did bodily eat or drink His body or blood, considering it was not then existing in nature but only was present to the believing heart by faith.

Objection 2. Another argument is taken from the words of the institution. "This is my body" (Luke 22:19). *Answer.* These words

---

15. In the margin: *Amala.* 2. *l. de off. Eccles. c.*12 & 15.

16. In the margin: *Lib. de expos. Liturg. cap.* 26.

must not be understood properly, but by a figure, His body being put for the sign and seal of His body. It is objected that when any make their last wills and testaments, they speak as plainly as they can. Now in this Supper, Christ ratifies His last will and testament, and therefore He spoke plainly, without any figure. *Answer.* Christ here speaks plainly and by a figure also. For it has been always the usual manner of the Lord in speaking of the sacraments to give the name of the thing signified to the sign—as [in] Genesis 17:10, circumcision is called "the covenant of God," and in the next verse in the way of exposition, "the sign of the covenant." And [in] Exodus 12:11, the paschal lamb is called the angels passing by or over the houses of the Israelites, whereas indeed it was but a sign thereof. And "the rock was Christ" (1 Cor. 10:4), "the Passover was Christ" (1 Cor. 5:7). And the like phrase is to be found in the institution of this sacrament concerning the cup, which the papists themselves confess to be figurative when it is said, "This cup is the New Testament in my blood" (Luke 22:20), that is, a sign, seal, and pledge thereof. Again, the time when these words were spoken must be considered, and it was before the passion of Christ, whereas yet His body was not crucified nor His blood shed. And consequently, neither of them could be received in bodily manner, but by faith alone. Again, Christ was not only the author, but the minister of this sacrament at the time of institution thereof, and if the bread had been truly turned into His body and the wine into His blood, Christ with His own hands should have taken His own body and blood and have given it to His disciples. No, which is more, He should, with His own hands, have taken His own flesh, and drunk His own blood, and have eaten Himself. For Christ Himself did eat the bread and drink the wine that He might with His own person consecrate His Last Supper, as He had consecrated baptism before. And if these words should be properly understood, every man should be a manslayer in his eating of Christ. Lastly, by means of popish real presence, it comes to pass that our bodies should be nourished by naked qualities without any substance, which in all philosophy is false and erroneous. To help this and the like absurdities, some papists make nine wonders in the sacrament: "The first, that Christ's body is in the eucharist in as large a quantity as He was upon the cross, and is now in heaven, and yet excludes not the quantity of the bread. The second, that there be accidents without a subject. The third, that bread is turned into the body of Christ, and yet it is not the matter of the body, nor resolved to nothing. The fourth, that the body increases not by consecration of many hosts and is not diminished by often receiving. The fifth, that the body of Christ is under many consecrated hosts. The sixth, that when the host is divided, the body of Christ is not divided, but under every part thereof is whole Christ. The seventh, that when the priest holds the host in his hand, the body of Christ is not felt by itself nor seen, but the forms of bread and wine. The eighth, that when the forms of bread and wine cease, the body and blood of Christ cease also to be there. The ninth, that the accidents of bread and wine have the same effects with the bread and wine itself, which are to nourish and fill."[17] On this manner it shall be easy for any man to defend the most absurd opinion that is or can be, if he may have liberty to answer the arguments alleged to the contrary by wonders.

To conclude, seeing there is a real communion in the sacrament between Christ and every believing heart, our duty therefore is to bestow our hearts on Christ, endeavoring to love Him, and to rejoice in Him, and to long after Him above all things. All our affiance must be in Him and with Him—we being now on

17. In the margin: *Io. De Combis comp. Theolog. l.* 6. *cap.* 14.

earth must have our conversation in heaven. And this is the true real presence which the ancient church of God has commended unto us. For in all these liturgies these words are used, and are yet extant in the popish mass, "Lift up your hearts; we lift them up unto the Lord." By which words the communicants were admonished to direct their minds and their faith to Christ sitting at the right hand of God. Thus says Augustine, "If we celebrate the ascension of the Lord with devotion, let us ascend with Him, and lift up our hearts."[18] Again, "They which are already risen with Christ in faith and hope, are invited to the great table of heaven, to the table of angels, *where is the bread*."[19]

18. In the margin: *Serm. de Ascens.* 1.

19. In the margin: *Serm.* 14. 2. *fer. pascae.*

THE ELEVENTH POINT

Of the Sacrifice in the Lord's Supper, which the Papists Call the Sacrifice of the Mass

Touching this point, first I will set down what must be understood by the name sacrifice. A sacrifice is taken properly or improperly. Properly it is a sacred or solemn action in which man offers and consecrates some outward bodily thing unto God for this end, to please and honor Him thereby. Thus, all the sacrifices of the Old Testament, and the oblation of Christ upon the cross in the New Testament, are sacrifices. Improperly, that is, only by the way of resemblance, the duties of the moral law are called sacrifices. And in handling this question I understand a sacrifice both properly and improperly by way of resemblance.

Our Consent

Our consent, I propound in two conclusions:[1]

Conclusion 1. That the Supper of the Lord is a sacrifice and may truly be so called as it has been in former ages, and that in three respects: 1. Because it is a memorial of the real sacrifice of

1. This paragraph break is not in the original.

Christ upon the cross and contains withal a thanksgiving to God for the same, which thanksgiving is the sacrifice and "calves of our lips" (Heb. 13:15). 2. Because every communicant there presents himself body and soul, a living, holy, and acceptable sacrifice unto God. For as in this sacrament God gives unto us Christ with His benefits, so we answerably give ourselves unto God as servants to walk in the practice of all dutiful obedience. 3. It is called a sacrifice in respect of that which was joined with the sacrament, namely, the alms given to the poor as a testimony of our thankfulness unto God. And in this regard also, the ancient fathers have called the sacrament *an unbloody sacrifice*; and the table, *an altar*; and the ministers, *priests*; and the whole action an *oblation*, not to God but to the congregation, and not by the priest alone, but by the people. A canon of a certain council says, "We decree that every Lord's Day the oblation of the altar be offered of every man and woman both for bread and wine."[2] And Augustine says that "women offer a sacrifice at the altar of the Lord, that it might be offered by the priest to God."[3] And usually in ancient writers the communion of the whole body of the congregation is called the sacrifice or oblation.

Conclusion 2. That the very body of Christ is offered in the Lord's Supper. For as we take the bread to be the body of Christ sacramentally by resemblance, and no otherwise, so the breaking of bread is sacramentally the sacrificing or offering of Christ upon the cross. And thus the fathers have termed the eucharist an immolation of Christ, because it is a commemoration of His sacrifice upon the cross. Augustine, *Epist.* 23, "Neither does he lie which says Christ was offered. For if sacraments had not the resemblance of things whereof they are sacraments, they should in no wise be sacraments. But from a resemblance, they often take

2. In the margin: *Concil. Matisc.* 2. *c.* 2.

3. In the margin: *Epist.* 122.

their names." Again, Christ is sacrificed in the Last Supper in regard of the faith of the communicants, which makes a thing past and done as present. Augustine says, "When we believe in Christ, He is offered for us daily." And, "Christ is then slain for everyone, when he believes that He is slain for him."[4] Ambrose says, "Christ is sacrificed daily in the minds of believers as upon an altar."[5] Jerome says, "He is always offered to the believers."[6]

II. The Difference

They make the eucharist to be a real, external, or bodily sacrifice offered unto God, holding and teaching that the minister is a priest properly, and that in this sacrament he offers Christ's body and blood to God the Father really and properly under the forms of bread and wine. We acknowledge no real, outward, or bodily sacrifice for the remission of sins, but only Christ's oblation on the cross once offered. Here is the main difference between us, touching this point. And it is of that weight and moment, that they stiffly maintaining their opinion (as they do) can be no church of God. For this point razes the foundation to the very bottom. And that it may the better appear that we avouch the truth, first, I will confirm our doctrine by Scripture, and second, confute the reasons which they bring for themselves.

III. Our Reasons

Reason 1. [Heb. 9:15, 26; 10:10.] The Holy Ghost says Christ offered Himself but once, therefore not often. And thus there can be no real or bodily offering of His body and blood in the sacrament of His Supper. The text is plain. The papists answer thus: "The sacrifice of Christ," say they, "is one for substance, yet in

---

4. In the margin: *Lib. 2. Quaest. Vet. & Nov. Test. Ad Rom.*

5. In the margin: *Lib. 2 de Virg.*

6. In the margin: *Ad Damas.*

regard of the manner of offering, it is either bloody or unbloody, and the Holy Ghost speaks only of the bloody sacrifice of Christ, which was indeed offered but once." *Answer.* But the author of the epistle takes it for granted that the sacrifice of Christ is only one, and that a bloody sacrifice. For he says, "Christ did not offer Himself often, as the high priests did" (Heb. 9:25), and "For then he must have often suffered since the foundation of the world: but now in the end he hath appeared once to put away sin by the sacrifice of himself" (v. 26). And, "*without shedding of blood* is no remission of sins" (v. 22). By these words, it is plain that the Scripture never knew the twofold manner of sacrificing of Christ. And every distinction in divinity not founded in the written Word is but a forgery of man's brain. And if this distinction be good, how shall the reason of the apostle stand, "He did not offer himself but once, because He suffered but once?"

Reason 2. The Romish Church holds that the sacrifice in the Lord's Supper is all one for substance, with[7] the sacrifice which He offered on the cross. If that be so, then the sacrifice in the eucharist must either be a continuance of that sacrifice which was begun on the cross, or else an alteration or repetition of it. Now let them choose of these two which they will. If they say it is a continuance of the sacrifice on the cross, Christ being but the beginner, and the priest the finisher thereof, they make it imperfect. For to continue a thing until it be accomplished is to bring perfection unto it. But Christ's sacrifice on the cross was then fully perfected, as by His own testimony it appears when He said, *Consummatum est,* "It is finished" (John 19:30). Again, if they say it is a repetition of Christ's sacrifice, thus also they make it imperfect—for that is the reason which the Holy Ghost uses to prove that the sacrifices of the Old Testament were imperfect, because they were repeated.

7. The 1635 edition incorrectly has *which* instead of *with.*

Reason 3. A real and outward sacrifice in a sacrament is against the nature of a sacrament, and especially the Supper of the Lord; for one end thereof is to keep in memory the sacrifice of Christ. Now every remembrance must be of a thing absent, past, and done. And if Christ be daily and really sacrificed, the sacrament is no fit memorial of His sacrifice. Again, the principal end for which the sacrament was ordained is that God might give and we receive Christ with His benefits. And therefore, to give and take, to eat and drink, are here the principal actions. Now in a real sacrifice God does not give Christ and the priest receive Him of God; but contrariwise he gives and offers Christ unto God, and God receives something of us. To help the matter, they say that this sacrifice serves not properly to make any satisfaction to God, but rather to apply unto us the satisfaction of Christ being already made. But this answer still goes against the nature of a sacrament, in which God gives Christ unto us. Whereas, in a sacrifice, God receives from man and man gives something to God. A sacrifice, therefore, is no fit means to apply anything unto us that is given of God.

Reason 4. [Heb. 7:24–25.] The Holy Ghost makes a difference between Christ, the high priest of the New Testament, and all Levitical priests, in this: that they were many, one succeeding another; but He is only one, having an eternal priesthood which cannot pass from Him to any other. Now if this difference be good, then Christ alone in His own very Person must be the priest of the New Testament, and no other with or under Him. Otherwise in the New Testament there should be more priests in number than in the Old. If they say that the whole action remains in the Person of Christ, and that the priest is but an instrument under Him (as they say), I say again it is false. Because the whole oblation is acted or done by the priest himself—and He which does all is more than a bare instrument.

Reason 5. If the priest offers to God Christ's real body and blood for the pardon of our sins, then man is become a mediator between God and Christ. Now the Church of Rome says that the priest—in his mass—is a priest properly, and his sacrifice a real sacrifice, differing only in the manner of offering from the sacrifice of Christ upon the cross. And in the very canon of the mass they insinuate thus much when they request "God to accept their gifts and offerings," namely, Christ Himself offered as He did the sacrifices of Abel and Noah. Now it is absurd to think that any creature should be a mediator between Christ and God. Therefore, Christ cannot possibly be offered by any creature unto God.

Reason 6. The judgment of the ancient church. A certain counsel held at Toledo in Spain reproved the ministers that they offered sacrifice often the same day without the holy communion. The words of the canon are these: "Relation is made unto us that certain priests do not so many times receive the grace of the holy communion, as they offer sacrifices in one day; but in one day, if they offer many sacrifices to God in all the oblations, they *suspend* themselves from the communion...."[8] Here mark, that the sacrifices in ancient masses were nothing else but forms of divine service—because none did communicate, no not the priest himself. And in another council, the name of the mass is put only for a form of prayer: "It has pleased us, that prayers, supplications, masses, which shall be allowed in the council...be used."[9] And in this sense it is taken when speech is used of the making or compounding of masses, for the sacrifice propitiatory of the body and blood of Christ admits no composition.[10] Abbot Paschaesius says, "Because we sin daily, Christ is sacrificed for us *mystically*, and His passion is

8. In the margin: *Tolet. Concil.* 12. *c.* 5.

9. In the margin: *Milevet. c.* 12.

10. In the margin: *Concil. Tol.* 4 *cap.* 12 & *Iacob de consecr. dist.* 1.

given in mystery."[11] These his words are against the real sacrifice, but yet he expounds himself more plainly, [in] *cap.* 10, "The blood is drunk in *mystery spiritually.*" And, "it is all *spiritual* which we eat." And [in] *cap.* 12, "The priest...distributes to everyone not as much as the outward sight gives, but as much as *faith receives,*"[12] [and in] *cap.* 13, "The *full* similitude is outwardly, and the immaculate flesh of the lamb is *faith inwardly*...that the truth be not wanting to the sacrament, and it be not ridiculous to pagans that we drink the blood of a killed man." [And in] *cap.* 6, "One eats the flesh of Christ spiritually and drinks His blood, another seems to receive not so much as a morsel of bread from the hand of the priest." His reason is because they come unprepared. Now then considering all these places, he makes no receiving but spiritual, neither does he make any sacrifice but spiritual.

IV. Objections of Papists

Objection 1. [Gen. 14:18.] When Abraham was coming from the slaughter of the kings, Melchizedek met him and brought forth bread and wine; and he was a priest of the most high God. "Now this bread and wine," say they, "he brought forth to offer for a sacrifice; because it is said he was a priest of the most high God." And they reason thus: "Christ was a priest after the order of Melchizedek; therefore, as Melchizedek offered bread and wine, so Christ under the forms of bread and wine offers Himself in sacrifice unto God." *Answer.* Melchizedek was no type of Christ in regard of the act of sacrificing, but in regard of his person, and things pertaining thereto, which all[13] are fully expounded [in] Hebrews 7, the sum whereof is this: 1. Melchizedek was both king and priest; so was Christ.

---

11. In the margin: *Lib. de corpor. & sang. dom. cap.* 9.

12. The 1635 edition incorrectly has *inwardly* instead of *receives.*

13. The 1635 edition omits the word *all.*

2. He was a prince of peace and righteousness; so was Christ. 3. He had neither father nor mother—because the Scripture in setting down his history makes no mention either of beginning or ending of his days—and so Christ had neither father nor mother. No father, as He was man; no mother, as He was God.

Melchizedek, being greater than Abraham, blessed him, and Christ, by virtue of His priesthood, blesses—that is justifies and sanctifies—all those that be of the faith of Abraham. In these things only stands the resemblance, and not in the offering of bread and wine. Again, the end of bringing forth the bread and wine was not to make a sacrifice, but to refresh Abraham and his servants that came from the slaughter of the kings. And he is called there a priest of the most high God, not in regard of any sacrifice, but in consideration of his blessing of Abraham, as the order of the words teaches: "And he was the priest of the most high God, and therefore he blessed him." Third, though it were granted that he brought forth bread and wine to offer in sacrifice, yet will it not follow that in the sacrament, Christ Himself is to be offered unto God under the naked forms of bread and wine. Melchizedek's bread and wine were absurd types of no-bread and no-wine, or of forms of bread and wine in the sacrament.

Objection 2. The paschal lamb was both a sacrifice and a sacrament. Now the eucharist comes in room thereof. *Answer.* The paschal lamb was a sacrament but no sacrifice. Indeed, Christ says to His disciples, "Go and prepare a place to sacrifice the Passover in" (Mark 14:12), but the words *to offer*, or to *sacrifice*, do often signify no more but *to kill.* As when Jacob and Laban made a covenant, it is said, "Jacob sacrificed beasts, and called his brethren to eat bread" (Gen. 31:54). Which words must not be understood of killing for sacrifice, but of killing for a feast—because he could not in good conscience invite them to his sacrifice that were out of the covenant, being (as they were) of another religion. Second, it may be called a sacrifice because it was killed after the manner of a sacrifice. Third, when Saul sought his father's asses and asked for the seer, a maid bids him go up in haste: "For," says she, "there is an offering of the people this day in the high place" (1 Sam. 9:12), where the feast that was kept in Rama is called a sacrifice; in all likelihood because at the beginning thereof, the priest offered a sacrifice to God. And so the Passover may be called a sacrifice because sacrifices were offered within the compass of the appointed feast or solemnity of the Passover [Deut. 16:2]; and yet the thing itself was no more a sacrifice than the feast in Rama was. Again, if it were granted that the Passover was both, it will not make much against us, for the Supper of the Lord succeeds the Passover only in regard of the main end thereof, which is the increase of our communion with Christ.

Objection 3. [Mal. 1:11.] "The prophet foretells of a clean sacrifice that shall be in the New Testament. And that," say they, "is the sacrifice of the mass." *Answer.* This place must be understood of a spiritual sacrifice, as we shall plainly perceive if we compare it with 1 Timothy 2:8, where the meaning of the prophet is fitly expounded: "I will," says Paul, "that men pray in all places, *lifting up pure hands* without wrath or doubting." And this is the clean sacrifice of the Gentiles. Thus, Justin Martyr says that "supplications and thanksgivings are the *only* perfect sacrifices pleasing God, and that Christians have learned to *offer them alone.*"[14] And Tertullian says, "We sacrifice for the health of the Emperor...as God has commanded with pure prayer."[15] And Irenaeus says that this clean offering to be offered in every place is the prayer of the saints.[16]

---

14. In the margin: *Dialog. cum Triph.*

15. In the margin: *Ad Scapulam.*

16. In the margin: *Lib.* 4 *c.* 35.

Objection 4: "We have an altar, whereof they may not eat, which serve in the tabernacle" (Heb. 13:10). "Now," say they, "if we have an altar, then we must needs have a priest; and also a real sacrifice." *Answer.* Here is meant not a bodily, but a spiritual altar, because the altar is opposed to the material tabernacle. And what is meant thereby is expressed in the next verse, in which he proves that we have an altar: "The bodies of the beasts, whose blood was brought into the holy place by the high priest for sin, were burnt without the camp; so Christ Jesus, that He might sanctify the people with His own blood, suffered without the gate" [vv. 11–12]. Now lay the reason or proof to the thing that is proved, and we must needs understand Christ Himself, who was both the altar, the priest, and the sacrifice.

Objection 5. Lastly, they say, where alteration is both of law and covenant, there must needs be a priest and a new sacrifice. But in the New Testament there is alteration both of law and covenant, and therefore there is both new priest and new sacrifice. *Answer.* All may be granted: In the New Testament there is both new priest and sacrifice, yet not any popish priest but only Christ Himself both God and man. The sacrifice also is Christ as He is man. And the altar Christ, as He is God, who in the New Testament offered Himself a sacrifice to His Father for the sins of the world. For though He was the Lamb of God slain from the beginning of the world, in regard of the purpose of God, in regard of the value of His merit, and regard of faith which makes things to come, as present, yet was He not actually offered until the fullness of time came. And once offering of Himself, He remains a priest forever, and all other priests beside Him are superfluous, His one offering once offered, being all-sufficient.

THE TWELFTH POINT

Of Fasting

I. Our Consent

Our consent may be set down in three conclusions:[1]

Conclusion 1. We do not condemn fasting, but maintain three sorts thereof: to wit, a moral, civil, and a religious fast. The first being moral, is a practice of sobriety or temperance, when as in the use of meats and drinks the appetite is restrained that it does not exceed moderation. And this must be used of all Christians in the whole course of their lives. The second being civil, is when upon some particular and politic considerations, men abstain from certain meats; as in this our commonwealth the law enjoins us to abstain from meat at certain seasons of the year for these special ends: to preserve the breed of cattle, and to maintain the calling of the fisherman. The third, namely a religious fast, is when the duties of religion, as the exercise of prayer and humiliation, are practiced in fasting. And I do now especially entreat of this kind.

1. This paragraph break is not in the original.

Conclusion 2. We join with them in the allowance of the principal and right ends of a religious fast, and they are three: The first is, that thereby the mind may become attentive in meditation of the duties of godliness to be performed. The second is, that the rebellion of the flesh may be subdued—for the flesh pampered becomes an instrument of licentiousness. The third, and (as I take it) the chief end of a religious fast, is to profess our guiltiness and to testify our humiliation before God for our sins. And for this end, in the fast of Nineveh, the very beast was made to abstain.

Conclusion 3. We yield unto them that fasting is a help and furtherance to the worship of God—yes, and a good work also if it be used in a good manner. For though fasting in itself being a thing indifferent—as eating and drinking are—is not to be termed a good work; yet being applied, and considered in relation to the right ends before spoken of and practiced accordingly, it is a work allowed of God and highly to be esteemed of all the servants and people of God.

II. The Dissent or Difference

Our dissent from the Church of Rome in the doctrine of fasting stands in three things:[2]

[First,] they appoint and prescribe set times of fasting as necessary to be kept. But we hold and teach that to prescribe the time of a religious fast is in the liberty of the church and the governors thereof, as special occasion shall be offered. When the disciples of John asked Christ why they and the Pharisees fast often, but His disciples fasted not, He answered, "Can the children of the marriage chamber mourn as long as the bridegroom is with them? But the days will come when the bridegroom shall be taken away from them, *and then shall they fast*" (Matt. 9:15),

2. This paragraph break is not in the original.

where He gives them to understand that they must fast as occasions of mourning are offered. Where also I gather, that a set time of fasting is no more to be enjoined than a set time of mourning. It was the opinion of Augustine that "neither Christ nor His apostles appointed any times of fasting."[3] And Tertullian says that they of his time "fasted of their own accord freely, without law or commandment, as occasions and time served."[4] And Eusebius says that "Montanus was the first that made laws of fasting."[5] It is objected, that there is a set time of fasting prescribed in Leviticus 16:29. *Answer.* This set and prescribed fast was commanded of God as a part of the legal worship, which had his end in the death of Christ. Therefore, it does not justify a set time of fasting in the New Testament, where God has left man to his own liberty without giving the like commandment. It is again alleged that [in] Zechariah 7:5 there were set times appointed for the celebration of religious fasts unto the Lord—the fifth and the seventh months. *Answer.* They were appointed upon occasion of the present afflictions of the church in Babylon, and they ceased upon their deliverance. The like upon like occasion may we appoint. It is further objected that some churches of the Protestants observe set times of fasting. *Answer.* In some churches there be set days and times of fasting—not upon necessity, or for conscience's or religion's sake—but for politic or civil regards. Whereas, in the Romish Church it is held a mortal sin to defer the set time of fasting until the next day following.

Second, we dissent from the Church of Rome touching the manner of keeping a fast. For the best learned among them allow the drinking of wine, water, electuaries, and that often within the

---

3. In the margin: *Epist.* 86.

4. In the margin: *Contra Psychicos.*

5. In the margin: *Hist. l.* 5. *c.* 17.

compass of their appointed fast.[6] Yes, they allow the eating of one meal on a fasting day at noontide, and upon a reasonable cause one hour before the time of fasting not yet ended.[7] But this practice indeed is absurd and contrary to the practice of the Old Testament [Judg. 10:26; 1 Sam. 1:12]. Yes, it frustrates the end of fasting. For the bodily abstinence is an outward means and sign whereby we acknowledge our guiltiness and unworthiness of any of the blessings of God. Again, they prescribe a difference of meats, as white meat only to be used on their fasting days, and that of necessity—and for conscience's sake in most cases. But we hold this distinction of meats both to be foolish and wicked. Foolish, because in such meats as they prescribe, there is as much filling and delight as in any other meats—as namely in fish, fruits, wine, etc., which they permit. And it is against the end of a religious fast to use any refreshing at all, so far as necessity of health and comeliness will permit. Thus the church in times past used to abstain not only from meat and drink, but from all delights whatsoever, even from soft apparel and sweet ointments. "Sanctify a fast...let the *bridegroom go forth of his chamber* and the bride out of her bride chamber" (Joel 2:15). "I ate no *pleasant* bread, neither came *flesh nor wine* within my mouth, neither did I *anoint* myself at all, till three weeks of days were fulfilled" (Dan. 10:3). "Defraud not one another, *except* it be with consent for a time, that ye may give yourselves to *fasting* and prayer" (1 Cor. 7:5).

Again, we hold this practice to be wicked because it takes away the liberty of Christians, by which "unto the pure all things are pure" (Titus 1:15). And the apostle, [in] Galatians 5, bids us to "stand fast in this liberty," which the Church of Rome would thus abolish. For the better understanding of this, let us consider how the Lord Himself has from the beginning kept in His own hands,

6. In the margin: *Mola. Tract.* 3. *c.* 11.

7. In the margin: *Navar. c.* 21 *num.* 27.

as a master in His own house, the disposition of His creatures for the use of man, that he might depend on Him and His Word for temporal blessings. In the first age, He appointed unto him for meat every herb of the earth bearing seed, and every tree wherein there is the fruit of a tree bearing seed [Gen. 1:27]. And as for flesh, whether God gave unto him liberty to eat or not to eat, we hold it uncertain. After the flood, the Lord renewed His grant of the use of the creatures and gave His people liberty to eat the flesh of living creatures—yet so as He made some things unclean and forbade the eating of them; among the rest, the eating of blood. But since the coming of Christ, He has enlarged His Word and given liberty to all—both Jews and Gentiles—to eat of all kinds of flesh [Acts 10:13, 15]. This Word of His we rest upon; holding it a doctrine of devils for men to command an abstinence from meats for conscience's sake which the Lord Himself has created to be received with thanksgiving [1 Tim. 4:4]. Socrates, a Christian historiographer, says that, "The apostles left it free to everyone to use what kind of meat they would on fasting days and other times. Spiridion, in lent, dressed swine's flesh and set it before a stranger, eating himself and bidding the stranger also to eat; who refusing and professing himself to be a Christian, 'Therefore,' says he, 'the rather must you do it; for to the pure all things are pure, as the Word of God teaches us.'"[8]

Objection 1. But they object, Jeremiah 35, where Jonadab commanded the Rechabites to abstain from wine, which commandment they obeyed, and are commended for doing well in obeying of it. "Therefore," say they, "some kind of meats may lawfully be forbidden." *Answer.* Jonadab gave this commandment, not in way[9] of religion, or merit, but for other wise and politic

8. In the margin: *Trip hist. l.* 9. *c.* 37. *Hist. trip. l.* 1. *c.* 10.

9. The 1635 edition incorrectly has *awe* instead of *way.*

regards. For he enjoined his posterity not to drink wine, not to build houses, not to sow seed, or plant vineyards, or to have any in possession, but to live in tents—to the end they might be prepared to bear the calamities that should befall them in time to come. But the popish abstinence from certain meats has respect to conscience and religion; and therefore is of another kind, and can have no warrant thence.

Objection 2. [Dan. 10:3.] Daniel, being in heaviness for three weeks of days, abstained from flesh; and his example is our warrant. *Answer.* [First,] it was the manner of the holy men in ancient times, when they fasted many days together of their own accords, freely to abstain from sundry things—and thus Daniel abstained from flesh. But the popish abstinence from flesh is not free, but stands by commandment—and the omitting of it is a mortal sin. Again [second], if they will follow Daniel in abstaining from flesh, why do they not also abstain from all pleasant bread and wine, yes from ointments? And why will they eat anything in the time of their fast; whereas they cannot show that Daniel ate anything at all till evening? And Molanus has noted that our ancestors abstained from wine and dainties—and that some of them ate nothing for two or three days together.[10]

Objection 3. Third, they allege the diet of John the Baptist, whose meat was locusts and wild honey, and of Timothy, who abstained from wine. *Answer.* Their kind of diet and that abstinence which they used, was only for temperance's sake—not for conscience or to merit anything thereby. Let them prove the contrary if they can.

Third and lastly, we dissent from them touching certain ends of fasting. For they make abstinence itself in a person fitly prepared to be a part of the worship of God. But we take it to be a thing

---

10. In the margin: *Tract.* 3 *c.* 11 *conc.* 8.

indifferent in itself, and therefore no part of God's worship; and yet withal, being well used, we esteem it as a prop or furtherance of the worship in that we are made the fitter by it to worship God [Mark 7:6]. And hereupon some of the more learned sort of them say, "Not the work of fasting done, but the devotion of the worker, is to be reputed the service of God." Again, they say that "Fasting in—or with—devotion, is a work of satisfaction to God's justice for the temporal punishment of our sins." Wherein we take it they do blasphemously derogate from Christ our Savior, who is the whole and perfect satisfaction for sin, both in respect of fault and punishment. Here they allege the example of the Ninevites and Ahab's fasting, whereby they turned away the judgments of God denounced against them by His prophets. We answer, that God's wrath was appeased towards the Ninevites not by their fasting, but by faith laying hold on God's mercy in Christ, and thereby staying His judgment. Their fasting was only a sign of their repentance—their repentance a fruit and sign of their faith—whereby they believed the preaching of Jonah [Matt. 12:41]. As for Ahab's humiliation, it is nothing to the purpose. If they get anything thereby, let them take it to themselves. To conclude, we for our parts, do not condemn this exercise of fasting, but the abuse of it; and it were to be wished that fasting were more used of all Christians in all places, considering the Lord daily gives us new and special occasions of public and private fasting.

THE THIRTEENTH POINT

Of the State of Perfection

I. Our Consent

Our consent I will set down in two conclusions.[1]

Conclusion 1. All true believers have a state of true perfection in this life. "Be you perfect as your Father in heaven is perfect" (Matt. 5:48). "Noah was a just and perfect man in his time, and walked with God" (Gen. 6:9). "Walk before me and be perfect" (Gen. 17:1). And sundry kings of Judah are said to walk uprightly before God with a perfect heart, as David, Josias, Hezekiah, etc. And Paul accounts himself with the rest of the faithful to be perfect, saying, "Let us all that are perfect be thus minded" (Phil. 3:15). Now this perfection has two parts: The first is the imputation of Christ's perfect obedience, which is the ground and fountain of all our perfection whatsoever. "By one offering," that is, by His obedience in His death and passion, "has he consecrated," or made perfect, "forever them that believe" (Heb. 10:14). The second part of Christian perfection is sincerity, or uprightness, standing in two things: The first is, to

1. This paragraph break is not in the original.

acknowledge our imperfection and unworthiness in respect of ourselves. And hereupon, though Paul had said he was perfect, yet he adds further that he "did account of himself not as though he had attained to perfection—but did forget the good things behind and endeavored himself to that which was before" (Phil. 3:13, 15). Here therefore it must be remembered that the perfection whereof I speak may stand with sundry wants and imperfections. It is said of Asa that his "heart was perfect with God all his days" (1 Kings 15:14), and yet "he pulled not down the high places" (2 Chron. 15:17), and being diseased in his feet, "he put his trust in the physicians and not in the Lord" (2 Chron. 16:12). Second, this uprightness stands in a constant purpose, endeavor, and care to keep not some few, but all and every commandment of the law of God, as David says, "Then should I not be confounded, when I have respect to all thy commandments" (Ps. 119:6). And this endeavor is a fruit of perfection, in that it proceeds from a man regenerate. For as all men through Adam's fall have in them by nature the seeds of all sin—none excepted, no not the sin against the Holy Ghost—so by the grace of regeneration, through Christ, all the faithful have in them likewise the seeds of all virtues needful to salvation. And hereupon they both can and do endeavor to yield perfect obedience unto God according to the whole law. And they may be termed perfect, as a child is called a perfect man— though it want perfection of age and stature and reason—yet it has perfection of parts because it has all and every part and faculty both of body and soul that is required to [be] a perfect man.

Conclusion 2. There be certain works of supererogation—that is, such works as are not only answerable to the law and thereupon deserve life everlasting but go beyond the law and merit more than the law, by itself, can make any man to merit. But where may we find these works? Not in the person of any mere man or angel—nor in all men and angels—but only in the Person of Christ, God and man, whose works are not only answerable to the perfection of the law, but go far beyond the same. For first, the obedience of His life considered along by itself, was answerable even to the rigor of the law. And therefore, the sufferings of His death and passion were more than the law could require at His hand, considering it requires no punishment of Him that is a doer of all things contained therein. Second, the very rigor of the law required the obedience only of them that are mere men; but the obedience of Christ was the obedience of a Person that was both God and man. Third, the law requires personal obedience—that is, that every man fulfill the law for himself—and it speaks of no more. *Christ obeyed the law for Himself*, not because He did by His obedience merit His own glory—but because He was to be a perfect and pure high priest, not only in nature, but also in life. And as He was a creature, He was to be conformable to the law. Now the obedience which Christ performed was not for Himself alone, but it serves also for all the elect. And considering it was the obedience of God, as Paul signified when he said, "feed the church of God, which he purchased with his blood" (Acts 20:28), it was sufficient for many thousand worlds. And by reason, the law requires no obedience of Him that is God—this obedience, therefore, may truly be termed a work of supererogation. This one we acknowledge, and beside this we dare acknowledge none. And thus far we agree with the Church of Rome in the doctrine of the estate of perfection—and further we dare not go.[2]

II. The Difference

The papists hold (as the writings of the learned among them teach) that a man, being in the state of grace, may not only keep all the commandments of the law, and thereby deserve his own

2. The 1635 edition omits the word *go*.

salvation, but also go beyond the law, and do works of supererogation which the law requires not—as to perform the vow of single life, and the vow of regular obedience, etc. "And by this means," they say, "men deserve a greater degree of glory than the law can afford." Of perfection they make two kinds: One they call *necessary perfection*, which is the fulfilling of the law in every commandment, whereby eternal life is deserved. The second is *profitable perfection*, when men do not only such things as the law requires, but, over and besides, they make certain vows and perform certain other duties which the law enjoins not—for the doing whereof they shall be rewarded with a greater measure of glory than the law designs. This they make plain by comparison: Two soldiers fight in the field under one and the same captain. The one only keeps his standing and thereby deserves his pay; the other in keeping of his place, also wins the enemies' standard or does some other notable exploit. Now this man—besides his pay—deserves some greater reward. "And thus," say they, "it is with all true Catholics in the state of grace. They that keep the law shall have life eternal; but they that do more than the law, as works of supererogation, shall be crowned with greater glory." This is their doctrine. But we, on the contrary, teach that albeit we are to strive to a perfection as much as we can, yet no man can fulfill the law of God in this life, much less do works of supererogation. For the confirmation whereof, these reasons may be used:

Reason 1. In the moral law, two things are commanded. First, the love of God and man. Second, the manner of this love. Now the manner of loving God, is to love Him with all our heart and strength. "Thou shalt love the Lord thy God with all thy heart, and with all thy soul, and with all thy strength, and with all thy thought, etc." (Luke 10:27). As Bernard said, "the measure of loving God is to love Him without measure," and that is, to love Him with the greatest perfection of love that can befall a creature. Hence it follows, that in loving God, no man can possibly do more than the law requires. And therefore, the performance of all vows whatsoever, and all like duties, comes short of the intention or scope of the law.

Reason 2. The compass of the law is large and comprehends in it more than the mind of man can at the first conceive; for every commandment has two parts, the negative and the affirmative. In the negative is forbidden not only the capital sin named—as murder, theft, adultery, etc.—but all sins of the same kind with all occasions and provocations thereto. And in the affirmative is commanded not only the contrary virtues—as the love of God, and the love of our neighbor's honor, life, chastity, goods, good name—but the use of all helps and means whereby the said virtues may be preserved, furthered, and practiced. Thus has our Savior Christ Himself expounded the law [Matthew 5, 6]. Upon this plain ground I conclude that all duties pertaining to life and manners come within the list of some moral commandment. And that the papists—making their works of supererogation means to further the love of God and man—must needs bring them under the compass of the law. Under which, if they be, they cannot possibly go beyond the same.

Reason 3. "When we have done all those things that are commanded us, we are unprofitable servants: we have done that which was our duty to do" (Luke 17:10). The papists answer, that we are unprofitable to God but not to ourselves. But this shift of theirs is beside the very intent of the place. For a servant in doing his duty is unprofitable even to himself and does not so much as deserve thanks at his master's hand. As Christ says, "Does he thank that servant?" (v. 9). Second, they answer that we are unprofitable servants in doing things commanded, yet when we do things prescribed in the way of counsel, we may profit ourselves, and merit thereby. But this answer does not stand with reason. For things commanded, in that they are commanded, are more excellent than things left to our liberty, because the will and commandment of God gives excellency and goodness unto them. Again, counsels are thought to be harder than the commandments of the law. And if men cannot profit themselves by obedience of moral precepts, which are more easy, much less shall they be able to profit themselves by counsels, which are of greater difficulty.

Reason 4. If it be not in the ability and power of man to keep the law, then much less is he able to do any work that is beyond and above all the law requires. But no man is able to fulfill the law, and therefore no man is able to supererogate. Here the papists deny the proposition, "For," say they, "though we keep not the law yet we may do things of counsel above the law, and thereby merit." But by their leave, they speak absurdly. For in common reason, if a man fail in the less, he cannot but fail in the greater. Now (as I have said) in popish doctrine, it is easier to obey the moral law than to perform the counsels of perfection.

III. Objections of Papists

Objection 1. The Lord says, "Unto eunuchs that keep his Sabbath, and choose the thing that pleases him, will he give a place and name better than the sons and daughters" (Isa. 56:4). "Now," say they, "a eunuch is one that lives a single life and keeps the vow of chastity, and hereupon he is said to deserve a greater measure of glory." *Answer.* If the words be well considered, they prove nothing less. For honor is promised to eunuchs, not because they make and perform the vow of single life, but because (as the text says) they observe the Lord's Sabbath, and choose the thing that pleases God, and keep His covenant, which is, to believe the Word of God and to obey the commandments of the moral law.

Objection 2. Christ says, "There are some which have made themselves chaste for the kingdom of heaven" (Matt. 19:12). Therefore, the vow of single life is warrantable and is a work of special glory in heaven. *Answer.* The meaning of this text is that some having received the gift of continence, do willingly content themselves with single estate that they may with more liberty without distraction further the good estate of the church of God or the kingdom of grace in themselves and others. This is [all] that can be gathered out of this place—hence therefore cannot be gathered the merit of everlasting glory by single life.

Objection 3. Christ says to the young man, "If thou wilt be perfect, go sell that thou hast, and give to the poor, and thou shalt have treasure in heaven" (Matt. 19:21). "Therefore," say they, "a man by forsaking all, may merit not only heaven, but also treasure there—that is, an exceeding measure of glory." *Answer.* This young man, being in likelihood a most strict Pharisee, thought to merit eternal life by the works of the law, as his first question imparts: "Good master, what shall I do to be saved?" And therefore, Christ goes about to discover unto him the secret corruption of his heart. And hereupon the words alleged are a commandment of trial not common to all, but special to him. The like commandment gave the Lord to Abraham, saying, "Abraham take thine only son Isaac, and offer him upon the mountain which I shall show thee" (Gen. 22:2).

Objection 4. Paul says, "It is good for [all] to be single as he was" (1 Cor. 7:8). And he says, "It is better for virgins not to marry" (v. 38). And "this he speaks by permission, not by commandment" (v. 25). *Answer.* Here the single life is not preferred simply, but only in respect of the present necessity, because the church was then under persecution; and because such as live a single life are freed from the cares and distractions of the world.

Objection 5. [1 Cor. 9:15, 17, 18.] Paul preached the gospel freely, and that was more than he was bound to do—and for so doing he had a reward. *Answer.* It was generally in Paul's liberty to preach the gospel freely or not to do it. But in Corinth, upon special circumstances, he was bound in conscience to preach it freely as he did by reason of the false teachers, who would otherwise have taken occasion to disgrace his ministry and have hindered the glory of God.

Now it was Paul's duty by all means to prevent the hindrances of the gospel and the glory of God—and if he had not so done, he had abused his liberty (v. 18). Therefore, he did no more in that case than the law itself required. For an action indifferent, or an action in our liberty, ceases to be in our liberty and becomes moral in the case of offence. What is more free and indifferent than to eat flesh? Yet in the case of offence Paul said he "would not eat flesh as long as the world stood" (1 Cor. 8:13).

THE FOURTEENTH POINT

Of the Worshipping of Saints, Specially of Invocation

I. Our Consent

Conclusion 1. The true saints of God—as prophets, apostles, and martyrs, and such like—are to be worshipped and honored, and that [in] three ways:

By keeping a memory of them in godly manner. Thus the virgin Mary—as a prophetess—foretells that "all nations shall call her blessed" (Luke 1:48). When a certain woman poured a box of ointment on the head of Christ, He says, "this fact shall be spoken of in remembrance of her, wheresoever that gospel should be preached throughout the world" (Mark 14:9). This duty also was practiced by David towards Moses, Aaron, Phineas, and the rest that are commended (Psalms 105 and 106), and by the author of the epistle to the Hebrews upon the patriarchs and the prophets—and many others that excelled in faith in the times of the Old and New Testament. 2. They are to be honored by giving of thanks to God for them, and the benefits that God vouchsafed by them unto His church. Thus Paul says, that when the churches heard of his conversion, they "glorified God for him," or, "in him" (Gal. 1:23). And the like is to be done for the saints departed.

3. They are to be honored by an imitation of their faith, humility, meekness, repentance, the fear of God, and all good virtues wherein they excelled. For this cause, the examples of godly men in the Old and New Testament are called a "cloud of witnesses" by allusion. For as the cloud did guide the Israelites through the wilderness to the land of Canaan, so the faithful now are to be guided to the heavenly Canaan by the examples of good men that have believed in God before us and have walked the straight way to life everlasting.

Conclusion 2. Again, their *true relics*, that is, their virtues and good examples left to all posterity to be followed, we keep and respect with due reverence. Yes, if any man can show us the bodily relic of any true saint and prove it so to be, though we will not worship it, yet will we not despise it, but keep it as a monument if it may conveniently be done without offence. And thus far we consent with the Church of Rome. Further we must not go.

II. The Dissent

Our difference stands in the manner of worshipping of saints. The papists make two degrees of religious worship. The highest they call *latria,* whereby God Himself is worshipped and that alone. The second, lower than the former, is called *doulia*, whereby the saints and angels that be in the special favor of God, and glorified with everlasting glory in heaven, are worshipped. This worship they place in outward adoration, in bending of the knee, and bowing of the body to them being in heaven: in invocation whereby they call upon them; in dedication of churches and houses of religion unto them; in Sabbaths and festival days; lastly, in pilgrimages unto their relics and images. We likewise distinguish adoration or worship, for it is either religious or civil. Religious worship is that which is done to Him that is Lord of all things, the searcher and trier of the heart, omnipotent, everywhere present, able to hear and help them that call upon Him everywhere, the Author and first cause of every good[1] thing; and that simply for Himself because He is absolute goodness itself. And this worship is due to God alone, being also commanded in the first and second commandments of the first table. Civil worship is the honor done to men set above us by God Himself, either in respect of their excellent gifts or in respect of their offices and authority whereby they govern others. The right end of this worship is to testify and declare that we reverence the gifts of God and that power which He has placed in those that be His instruments. And this kind of worship is commanded only in the second table and in the first commandment thereof, "Honor thy father and mother" (Ex. 20:12). Upon this distinction we may judge what honor is due to everyone. Honor is to be given to God and to whom He commands. He commands that inferiors should honor or worship their betters. Therefore, the unreasonable creatures, and among the rest images, are not to be worshipped—either with civil or religious worship—being indeed far baser than man himself is. Again, unclean spirits, the enemies of God, must not be worshipped; yes, to honor them at all is to dishonor God. Good angels, because they excel men both in nature and gifts, when they appeared were lawfully honored; yet so, as when the least signification of honor was given that was proper to God, they refused it. And because they appear not now as in former times, not so much as civil adoration in any bodily gesture is to be done unto them. Lastly, governors and magistrates have civil adoration as their due, and it cannot be omitted without offence. Thus, Abraham worshipped the Hittites [Genesis 23] and Joseph his brethren [Genesis 50]. To come to the very point, upon the former distinction we deny against the papists that any civil worship in the bending of the knee or

1. The 1635 edition incorrectly has *God* instead of *good.*

prostrating of the body is to be given to the saints—they being absent from us—much less any religious worship, as namely invocation signified by any bodily adoration. For it is the very[2] honor of God Himself; let them call it *latria*, or *doulia*, or by what name they will.

Our Reasons

Reason 1. All true invocation and prayer made according to the will of God must have a double foundation: a commandment and a promise. A commandment, to move us to pray; and a promise, to assure us that we shall be heard. For all and every prayer must be made in faith; and without a commandment or promise, there is no faith. Upon this infallible ground I conclude that we may not pray to saints departed. For in the Scripture there is no word, either commanding us to pray unto them or assuring us that we shall be heard when we pray. No, we are commanded only to call upon God, "Him only shalt thou serve" (Matt. 4:10). And "how shall we call upon him in whom we have not believed?" (Rom. 10:14). And we have no promise to be heard, but for Christ's sake. Therefore, prayers made to saints departed are unlawful. Answer is made, that "Invocation of saints is warranted by miracles and revelations, which are answerable to commandments and promises." *Answer.* But miracles and revelations had an end before this kind of invocation took any place in the church of God—and that was about three hundred years after Christ. Again, to judge of any point of doctrine by miracles is deceitful unless three things concur: the first is, doctrine of faith and piety to be confirmed; the second is, prayer unto God, that something may be done for the ratifying of the said doctrine; the third is, the manifest edification of the church by the two former. Where any of these three are wanting, miracles may be suspected, because

2. The 1635 edition omits the word very.

otherwise false prophets have their miracles to try men whether they will cleave unto God or not [Deut. 13:1, 3]. Again, miracles are not done—or to be done—for them that believe, but for infidels that believe not. As Paul says, "Tongues are a sign, not to them that believe, but to unbelievers" (1 Cor. 14:22). And to this agree Chrysostom, Ambrose, and Isidore, who says, "Behold, a sign is not necessary to believers which have already believed, but to infidels, that they may be converted." Lastly, our faith is to be confirmed, not by revelation and apparitions of dead men, but by the writings of the apostles and prophets [Luke 16:29].

Reason 2. To pray unto saints departed—to bow the knee unto them while they are in heaven—is to ascribe that unto them which is proper to God Himself: namely, to know the heart with the inward desires and motions thereof, and to know the speeches and behaviors of all men in all places upon earth at all times. The papists answer that saints in heaven see and hear all things upon earth not by themselves (for that were to make them gods) but in God, and in the glass of the Trinity, in which they see men's prayers revealed unto them. I answer first, that the saints are still made more than creatures because they are said to know the thoughts and all the doings of all men at all times, which no created power can well comprehend at once. Second, I answer, that this glass, in which all things are said to be seen, is but a forgery of man's brain, and I prove it thus. The angels themselves, who see further into God than men can do, never knew all things in God, which I confirm on this manner: In the temple, under the law, upon the ark, were placed two cherubim, signifying the good angels of God. And they looked downward upon the mercy seat covering the ark, which was a figure of Christ. And their looking downward figured their desire to see into the mystery of Christ's incarnation and our redemption by Him; as Peter alluding, no doubt, to this type in the Old Testament says, "Which things the angels desire to behold" (1 Peter 1:12). And Paul says, "The manifold wisdom of God is revealed by the church unto principalities and powers in heavenly places" (Eph. 3:10), that is, to the angels. But how, and by what means? *By the church*, and that two ways: First, by the church, as by an example in which the angels saw the endless wisdom and mercy of God in the calling of the Gentiles. Second, by the church, as it was founded and honored by the preaching of the apostles. For it seems that the apostolical ministry in the New Testament revealed things touching Christ which the angels never knew before that time. Thus Chrysostom, upon occasion of this text of Paul, says that "The angels learned something by the preaching of John the Baptist."[3] Again, Christ says that "*they know not* the hour of the last judgment" (Matt. 24:36). Much less do the saints know all things in God. And hence it is that they are said to be under the altar where they cry, "How long, Lord, holy and true! Wilt thou not avenge our blood?" (Rev. 6:10), as being ignorant of the day of their full deliverance. And the Jews in affliction confess Abraham was ignorant of them and their estate [Isa. 63:16].

Reason 3. Christ refused so much as to bow the knee to Satan, upon this ground, because it was written, "Thou shalt worship the Lord thy God, and him only shalt thou serve" (Matt. 4:10). Hence it was that Peter would not suffer Cornelius so much as to kneel unto him, though Cornelius intended not to honor him as God. Therefore, neither saint nor angel is to be honored so much as with the bowing of the knee, if it carries but the least signification of divine or religious honor.

Reason 4. The judgment of the ancient church. Augustine, "We honor the saints with charity and not by *servitude*; neither do we erect churches to them." And, "Let it *not be religion* for us to

---

3. In the margin: *Prolog. in Ioh.*

worship dead men." And, "They are to be honored for imitation, and not to be adored for religion."[4] Epiphan., "Neither Thecla, nor any saint is to be adored, for that ancient *error* may not overrule us, that we should leave the living God, and adore things made by Him." Again, "Let Mary be in honor; let the Father, Son, and Holy Ghost be adored. Let *none adore* Mary—I mean neither woman nor man." Again, "Mary is beautiful, holy, and honored, yet *not to adoration*."[5] When Julian objected to the Christians that they worshipped their martyrs as God, Cyril grants the memory and honor of them, but denies their adoration. And of invocation he makes no mention at all.[6] Ambrose on Romans 1: "Is any so mad that he will give to the Earl the honor of the King?—yet these men do not think themselves guilty who give the honor of God's name to a creature, and leaving the Lord *adore their fellow servants*, as though there were anything more reserved for God."

III. Objections of Papists

Objection 1. "Let the angel that kept me bless thy children" (Gen. 48:16). "Here," say they, "it is a prayer made to angels." *Answer.* By the angel is meant Christ, who is called the angel of the covenant [Mal. 3:1], and the angel that guided Israel in the wilderness [1 Cor. 10:9 compared with Ex. 23:20].

Objection 2. [Ex. 32:13.] "Moses prays that God would respect His people, for Abraham's sake, and for Isaac and Israel His servants, which were not then living." *Answer.* Moses prays [for] God to be merciful to the people, not for the intercession of Abraham, Isaac, and Jacob, but for His covenant's sake which He had made with them [Ps. 132:10–11]. Again, by popish doctrine,

4. In the margin: *De vera relig. cap.* 35.

5. In the margin: *Haer.* 79.

6. In the margin: *Lib.* 9 & 10.

the fathers departed knew not the estate of men upon earth, neither did they pray for them—because then they were not in heaven but in *Limbo Patrum.*

Objection 3. "One living man makes intercession to God for another; therefore, much more do the saints in glory, that are filled with love, pray to God for us." *Answer.* The reason is naught—for we have a commandment, one living man to pray for another, and to desire others to pray for us. But there is no warrant in the Word of God for us to desire the prayers of men departed. Second, there is a great difference between these two: to request our friend—either by word of mouth or by letter—to pray for us, and by invocation to request them that are absent from us and departed this life to pray for us. For this is indeed a worship, in which is given unto them a power to hear and help all that call upon them at what place or time forever—yes, though they be not present in the place in which they are worshipped—and consequently, the seeing of the heart, presence in all places, and infinite power to help all that pray unto them, which things agree to no creature but God alone. Third, when one living man requests another to pray for him, he only makes him his companion and fellow member in his prayer made in the name of our Mediator, Christ. But when men invocate saints in heaven, they, being then absent, make them more than fellow members, even mediators between Christ and them.

THE FIFTEENTH POINT

Of Intercession of Saints

I. Our Consent

Our consent with them I will set down in two conclusions:[1]

Conclusion 1. The saints departed pray unto God by giving thanks unto Him for their own redemption, and for the redemption of the whole church of God upon earth. "The four beasts and the four and twenty elders fell down before the Lamb..." (Rev. 5:8); "and they sang a new song, Thou art worthy to take the book and to open the seals thereof, because thou wast killed and hast redeemed us to God..." (v. 9); "And all the creatures which are in heaven...heard I, saying, Praise and honor and glory and power be unto Him that sitteth upon the throne and unto the Lamb forevermore" (v. 13).

Conclusion 2. The saints departed pray generally for the state of the whole church. "And I saw under the altar the souls of them that were killed for the word of God...and they cried" (Rev. 6:9), "How long, Lord, holy and true! dost thou not judge and avenge our blood on them that dwell on the earth?" (v. 10).

1. This paragraph break is not in the original.

Whereby we see they desire a final deliverance of the church and a destruction of the enemies thereof; that they themselves with all the people of God, might be advanced to fullness of glory in body and soul. Yes, the dumb creatures are said to "groan and sigh, waiting for the adoption, even the redemption of our bodies" (Rom. 8:23). Much more then do the saints in heaven desire the same. And thus far we consent.

II. The Dissent or Difference

They hold and teach that the saints in heaven, as the virgin Mary, Peter, Paul, etc., do make intercession to God for particular men according to their several wants; and that having received particular men's prayers, they present them unto God. But this doctrine we flatly renounce upon these grounds and reasons:

Reason 1. The church says to God, "Doubtless thou art our father, though Abraham *be ignorant of us*, and Israel *know us not*" (Isa. 63:16). Now if Abraham knew not his posterity, neither Mary, nor Peter, nor any other of the saints departed know us and our estate; and consequently, they cannot make any particular intercession for us. If they say that Abraham and Jacob were then in *limbo*, which they will have to be a part of hell, what joy could Lazarus have in Abraham's bosom? [Luke 16:25]. And with what comfort could Jacob say on his death bed, "O Lord, I have waited for thy salvation" (Gen. 49:18)?

Reason 2. Huldah, the prophetess, tells Josiah, he "must be gathered to his fathers and put in his grave in peace, that his eyes may not see all the evil which God would bring on that place (2 Kings 22:20). Therefore, the saints departed see not the state of the church on earth, much less do they know the thoughts and prayers of men. This conclusion Augustine confirms at large.

Reason 3. No creature, saint, or angel can be a mediator for us to God, saving Christ alone, who is indeed the only Advocate of

His church. For in a true and sufficient mediator there must be three properties: First of all, the Word of God must reveal and propound him unto the church that we may in conscience be assured that praying to him and to God in his name we shall be heard. Now there is no Scripture that mentions either saints or angels as mediators in our behalf, save Christ alone. Second, a mediator must be perfectly just, so as no sin be found in him at all: "If any man sin, we have an advocate with the Father, Jesus Christ the righteous" (1 John 2:1). Now the saints in heaven, howsoever they be fully sanctified by Christ, yet in themselves they were conceived and born in sin, and therefore must needs eternally stand before God by the mediation and merit of another. Third, a mediator must be a propitiator, that is, bring something to God that may appease and satisfy the wrath and justice of God for our sins. Therefore, John adds, "and he is a *propitiation* for our sins." But neither saint nor angel can satisfy for the least of our sins; Christ only is the propitiation for them all. The virgin Mary and the rest of the saints, being sinners, could not satisfy so much as for themselves.

Reason 4. The judgment of the church. Augustine, "All Christian men commended each other in their prayers to God." And, "who *prays for all*, and for whom *none prays*, He is that one and true Mediator."[2] And, "This says your Savior, you have *nowhere* to go but to Me, you have no way to go but by Me."[3] Chrysostom, "You have *no need of patrons* to God or much discourse that you should sooth others. But though you be alone and want a patron, and by yourself pray unto God, you shall obtain your desire." And on the saying of John, "If any sin, etc.," "Your prayers have no effect unless they be such *as the Lord commends* unto your Father."[4]

2. In the margin: *Lib.* 3. *contra Parmen. c.* 3.

3. In the margin: *Tract in Ioh.* 22.

4. In the margin: *De perfectu Evang.*

And Augustine on the same place has these words, "He being such a man said not, 'you have an Advocate,' but if any sin 'we have'; he said not, 'you have,' neither said he, '*you have me.*'"

III. Objections of Papists

Objection 1. "The four and twenty elders fall down before the Lamb, having every one harps and golden vials full of odors, which are the prayers of the saints" (Rev. 5:8–9). Hence the papists gather that the saints in heaven receive the prayers of men on earth and offer them unto the Father. *Answer.* There, by prayers of the saints, are meant their own prayers, in which they sing praises to God and to the Lamb, as the verses following plainly declare. And these prayers are also presented unto God, only from the hand of the angel, which is Christ Himself [Rev. 8:4].

Objection 2. [Luke 16:17.] Dives, in hell, prays for his brethren upon earth; much more do the saints in heaven pray for us. *Answer.* Out of a parable nothing can be gathered, but that which is agreeable to the intent and scope thereof. For by the same reason it may as well be gathered that the soul of Dives, being in hell, had a tongue. Again, if it were true which they gather, we may gather also that the wicked in hell have compassion and love to their brethren on earth and a zeal to God's glory, all which are false.

Objection 3. The angels in heaven know every man's estate. They know when any sinner repents and rejoice thereat and pray for particular men [Luke 15:10]. Therefore, the saints in heaven do the like, for they are equal to the good angels [Luke 20:36]. *Answer.* The place in Luke is to be understood of the estate of holy men at the day of the last judgment, as appears [in] Matthew 22:30, where it is said, that the servants of God *in the resurrection* are as the angels in heaven. Second, they are like the angels, not in office and ministry—by which they are ministering spirits for the good of men—but they are like them in glory.

Second, we dissent from the papists because they are not content to say that the saints departed pray for us in particular; but they add further, that they make intercession for us by their merits in heaven. New Jesuits deny this, but let them hear Lombard: "I think," says he, speaking of one that is but of mean goodness, "that he—as it were, passing by the fire—shall be saved by the merits and intercessions of the heavenly church; which do always make intercession for the faithful by request and merit, until Christ shall be complete in His members."[5] And the Roman Catechism says as much: "Saints are so much the more to be worshipped and called upon, because they make prayers daily for the salvation of men; and God for their merit and favor bestows many benefits upon us."[6] We deny not that men upon earth have help and benefit by the faith and piety which the saints departed showed when they were in this life. For God shows mercy on them that keep His commandments to a thousand generations. And Augustine says it was good for the Jews that they were loved of Moses, whom God loved.[7] But we utterly deny that we are helped by merits of saints, either living or departed. For saints in glory have received the full reward of all their merits—if they could merit—and therefore, there is nothing further that they can merit.

5. In the margin: *Lib.* 4 *dist.* 45 *p.* 6.

6. In the margin: On the second command.

7. In the margin: *q.* 149. *super Exod.*

THE SIXTEENTH POINT

Of Implicit or Infolded[1] *Faith*

I. Our Consent

We hold that there is a kind of implicit or unexpressed faith. Yes, that the faith of every man in some part of his life, as in the time of his first conversion and in the time of some grievous temptation or distress, is implicit or infolded. The Samaritans are said to *believe* [John 4:14] because they took Christ for the Messiah, and thereupon were content to learn and obey the glad tidings of salvation. And in the same place [v. 53], the ruler, with his family, is said to believe, who did no more but generally acknowledge that Christ was the Messiah and yielded himself to believe and obey His holy doctrine, being moved thereunto by a miracle wrought upon his young son. And Rahab [Heb. 11:13] is said to believe, yea, she is commended for faith, even at the time when she received the spies. Now in the Word of God we cannot find that she had any more but a confused, general, or infolded faith, whereby she believed that the God of the Hebrews was the true God and His Word [was] to be obeyed. And this faith (as it

1. *Infolded*: implied or necessarily included in a thing.

seems) was wrought by her by the report and relation of the miracles done in the land of Egypt, whereby she was moved to join herself unto the people of God and to believe as they did. By these examples then, it is manifest that in the very servants of God there is and may be, for a time, an implicit faith. For the better understanding of this point, it is to be considered that faith may be infolded two ways: first, in respect of knowledge of things to be believed; second, in respect of the apprehension of the object of faith, namely, Christ and His benefits. Now faith is infolded in respect of knowledge when sundry things that are necessary to salvation are not as yet distinctly known. Though Christ commended the faith of His disciples for such a faith against which the gates of hell should not prevail, yet was it unexpressed or wrapped up in regard of sundry points of religion [Matt. 16:18]. For first of all, Peter that made confession of Christ in the name of the rest, was at that time ignorant of the particular means whereby his redemption should be wrought.

For after this, he went about to dissuade his master from the suffering of death at Jerusalem, whereupon Christ sharply rebuked him, saying, "Come behind me, Satan, thou art an offence unto me" (Matt. 16:23). Again, they were all ignorant of Christ's resurrection until certain women who first saw Him after He was risen again had told them—and they, by experience in the Person of Christ, had learned the truth. Third, they were ignorant of the ascension—for they dreamed of an earthly kingdom at the very time when He was about to ascend, saying, "Wilt thou at this time restore the kingdom of Israel?" (Acts 1:6). And after Christ's ascension, Peter knew nothing of the breaking down of the partition wall between the Jews and Gentiles until God had better schooled him in a vision [Acts 10:14].[2]

2. This paragraph break is not the original.

And no doubt, we have ordinary examples of this implicit faith in sundry persons among us. For some there be which are dull and hard both for understanding and memory and thereupon make no such proceedings in knowledge as many others do. And yet for good affection and conscience in their doings, so far as they know, they come not short of any; having withal a continual care to increase in knowledge and to walk in obedience according to that which they know. And such persons, though they be ignorant in many things, yet have they a measure of true faith—and that which is wanting in knowledge is supplied in affection. And in some respects, they are to be preferred before many that have the glib tongue and the brain swimming with knowledge. To this purpose Melanchthon said well, "We must acknowledge the great mercy of God, who puts a difference between sins of ignorance and such as are done wittingly; and forgives manifold ignorances to them that know but the foundation and be teachable; as may be seen by the apostles, in whom there was much want of understanding before the resurrection of Christ. But, as has been said, He requires that we be teachable, and He will not have us to be hardened in our sluggishness and dullness. As it is said, [in] Psalm 1, he meditates in His law, day and night."[3]

The second kind of implicit faith is in regard of apprehension; when as a man cannot say distinctly and certainly, "I believe the pardon of my sins," but, "I do unfeignedly desire to believe the pardon of them all, and I desire to repent." This case befalls many of God's children when they are touched in conscience for their sins. But where men are displeased with themselves for their offences, and do withal constantly from the heart desire to believe, and to be reconciled to God, there is faith and many other graces of God infolded—as in the

3. In the margin: *Epitom. Phil. moral. de grad. delict.*

little and tender bud is infolded the leaf, the blossom, and the fruit. For though a desire to repent and believe be not faith and repentance in nature, yet in God's acceptation it is, God accepting the will for the deed. Christ will not "quench the smoking flax" [Isa. 42:3], which as yet, by reason of weakness, gives neither light nor heat. Christ says, "Blessed are they that *hunger and thirst* after righteousness, for they shall be satisfied" (Matt. 5:6), whereby persons hungering and thirsting are meant all such as feel with grief their own want of righteousness, and withal desire to be justified and sanctified [Rom. 8:26]. God hears and regards the very groans and sighs of His servants. Yes, though they be unspeakable by reason, they are oftentimes little, weak, and confused; yet God has respect unto them, because they are the work of His own Spirit. Thus then, we see that in a touched heart desiring to believe, there is an infolded faith.[4]

And this is the faith which many of the true servants of God have. And our salvation stands not so much in our apprehending of Christ as in Christ's comprehending of us. And therefore, Paul says, "he follows," namely, "*after perfection*, if that he might comprehend that, for whose sake he is comprehended of Christ" (Phil. 3:12). Now if any shall say, that "without a lively faith in Christ none can be saved," I answer, that "God accepts the desire to believe for lively faith in the time of temptation and in the time of our first conversion," as I have said. Put case,[5] a man that never yet repented falls into some grievous sickness, and then begins to be touched in conscience for his sins and to be truly humbled. Hereupon he is exhorted to believe his own reconciliation with God in Christ and the pardon of his own sins. And as he is exhorted, so he endeavors according to the measure of grace received, to believe—yet after much striving he cannot resolve himself that

4. This paragraph break is not the original.

5. *Put case*: to suppose.

he distinctly and certainly believes the pardon of his own sins. Only this he can say, that he heartily desires to believe; this he wishes above all things in the world. And he esteems all things as dung for Christ, and thus he dies. I demand now, what shall we say of him? Surely, we may say nothing but that he died the child of God and is undoubtedly saved. For howsoever it were a happy thing if men could come to that fullness of faith which was in Abraham and many servants of God, yet certain it is that God in sundry cases accepts of this desire to believe for true faith indeed. And look, as it is in nature, so it is in grace. In nature, some die when they are children, some in old age, and some in full strength, and yet all die men. So again, some die babes in Christ, some of more perfect faith. And yet the weakest—having the seeds of grace—is the child of God; and faith in his infancy is faith. All this while, it must be remembered [that] I say not there is a true faith without all apprehension, but without a distinct apprehension for some space of time. For this very desire, by faith to apprehend Christ and His merits, is a kind of apprehension. And thus we see the kinds of implicit or infolded faith.

This doctrine is to be learned for two causes: first of all, it serves to rectify the consciences of weak ones, that they be not deceived touching their estate. For if we think that no faith can save but a full persuasion—such as the faith of Abraham was—many truly bearing the name of Christ must be put out of the roll of the children of God. We are therefore to know that [there is a growth in grace, as in nature. And][6] there be differences and degrees of true faith, and the least of them all is this infolded faith. This in effect is the doctrine of master Calvin: that when we begin by faith to know somewhat and have a desire

6. The words, "there is growth in grace, as in nature. And," are not in the 1635 edition.

to learn more, this may be termed an unexpressed faith.[7] Second, this point of doctrine serves to rectify and in part to expound sundry catechisms, in that they seem to propound faith unto men at so high a reach as few can attain unto it; defining it to be a certain and full persuasion of God's love and favor in Christ; whereas though every faith be for his nature a certain persuasion, yet only the strong faith is the full persuasion. Therefore, faith is not only in general terms to be defined, but also the degrees and measures thereof are to be expounded, that weak ones—to their comfort—may be truly informed of their estate. And though we teach there is a kind of implicit faith, which is the beginning of true and lively faith, yet none must hereupon take an occasion to content themselves therewith, but labor to increase and go on from faith to faith. And so indeed will everyone do that has any beginnings of true faith, be they never so little. And he which thinks he has a desire to believe and contents himself therewith, has indeed no true desire to believe.

II. The Difference

The pillars of the Romish Church lay down this ground: that faith in his own nature is not a knowledge of things to be believed, but a reverent assent unto them, whether they be known or unknown. Hereupon they build: that if a man knows some necessary points of religion, as the doctrine of the Godhead, of the Trinity, of Christ's incarnation, and of our redemption, etc., it is needless to know the rest by a particular or distinct knowledge, and it suffices to give his consent to the church, and to believe as the pastors believe. Behold a ruinous building upon a rotten foundation. For faith contains a knowledge of things to be believed, and knowledge is of the nature of faith. And nothing is believed that is not known: "The knowledge of my righteous servant

7. In the margin: *Instit. Lib.* 3, *c.* 2, *Sect.* 5.

shall justify many" (Isa. 53:11). "This is eternal life, to know thee, the eternal God, and whom thou hast sent, Jesus Christ" (John 17:3). In these places, by knowledge is meant faith grounded upon knowledge, whereby we know, and are assured that Christ and His benefits belong unto us. Second, this kind of assent is the mother of ignorance. For when men shall be taught that for sundry points of religion they may believe as the church believes—that the study of the Scriptures is not to be required of them; yes, that to their good they may be barred the reading of them, so be it they know some principal things contained in the articles of faith[8]—that common believers are not bound expressly to believe all the articles of the Apostles' Creed[9]—that it suffices them to believe the articles by an implicit faith, by believing as the church believes: few or none will have care to profit in knowledge.[10] And yet God's commandment is that we should grow in knowledge, and that His Word should dwell plenteously in us [Col. 3:16]. Again, the papists say that the devotion of the ignorant is often service better accepted than that which is done upon knowledge. "Such," say they, "as pray in Latin pray with as great consolation of spirit, with as little tediousness, with as great devotion and affection, and oftentimes more than the other, and always more than any schismatic or heretic in his own language."[11] To conclude, they teach that some articles of faith are believed generally of the whole church only by a simple or implicit faith, which afterward by the authority of a general council are propounded to be believed of the church by express faith.[12] Roffensis, against Luther, gives an

8. In the margin: *Mol. tract.* 3, *c.* 27, *conclus.* 15.

9. In the margin: Bonav. & Durand.

10. In the margin: Bannes 2. *q.* 2 *art.* 7 ascribes this opinion to *Gul. Pariensis,* & to Altisiodorensis.

11. In the margin: *Rhem. Testam.* 1 Cor. 14.

12. In the margin: *Mol. Tract* 5 *c.* 30 *conclus.* 12.

example of this when he confesses that purgatory was little known at the first, but was made known partly by Scripture, and partly by revelation in process of time.[13] This implicit faith touching articles of religion we reject, holding that all things concerning faith and manners necessary to salvation are plainly expressed in Scripture, and accordingly, to be believed.

13. In the margin: *Contra affer. Lut. art.* 8.

THE SEVENTEENTH POINT

Of Purgatory

I. Our Consent

We hold a Christian purgatory, according as the Word of God has set down the same unto us. And first of all, by this purgatory we understand the afflictions of God's children here on earth [Lam. 1]. The people afflicted say, "Thou hast sent a fire into our bones. We have gone through water and fire" (Ps. 65:12). The children of Levi must be "purified in a purging fire" of affliction (Mal. 3:3). Afflictions are called "the fiery trial," whereby men are cleansed from their corruption, as gold from the dross by the fire (1 Peter 1:7). Second, the blood of Christ is a purgatory of our sins. "Christ's blood *purgeth* us from all our sins" (1 John 1:7). "It *purgeth* our consciences *from dead works*" (Heb. 9:14). And Christ "baptizes with the Holy Ghost *and with fire*" (Matt. 3:11), because our inward washing is by the blood of Christ. And the Holy Ghost is as fire, to consume and abolish the inward corruption of nature. To this effect says Origen, "Without doubt, we shall feel the unquenchable fire, unless we shall now entreat the Lord to send down *from heaven a purgatory fire* unto us, whereby worldly desires may be utterly consumed in our minds."[1] Augustine, "Suppose the *mercy* of God is *your purgatory*."[2]

II. The Difference or Dissent

We differ from the papists touching purgatory in two things:

And first of all, for the place. They hold it to be a part of hell, into which an entrance is made only after this life. We for our parts deny it as having no warrant in the Word of God, which mentions only two places for men after this life—heaven and hell—with the two-fold condition thereof—joy and torment [Luke 16:25–26; John 3:36; Rev. 20:14–15; and 21:7–8; Matt. 8:11]. No, we find the contrary. They that die in the Lord are said "to rest from their labors" (Rev. 14:13), which cannot be true if any of them go to purgatory. And to cut off all cavils, it is further said, "their works," that is, the reward of their works, "follow them," even at the heels, as an acolyte or servant does his master. Augustine says well, "After this life there remains no compunction or *satisfaction*."[3] And, "Here is all remission of sin. Here be temptations that move us to sin. Lastly, here is the evil from which we desire to be delivered. But there is none of all these."[4] And, "We are not here without sin but we shall *go hence without sin*."[5] Cyril says, "They which are once dead can add nothing to the things which they have done, but shall *remain as they were left*, and wait for the time of the last judgment."[6] Chrysostom, "After the end of this life there be *no occasions* of merits."[7]

1. In the margin: *In Levit. l.* 9 *apud. Cyril.*
2. In the margin: *De Act. Faelic. c.* 21.
3. In the margin: *Hom.* 50. *tom.* 10.
4. In the margin: *Enchir. c.* 115.
5. In the margin: *De verb. Apost. serm.* 31.
6. In the margin: *lib.* 3 *in Es.*
7. In the margin: *Ad pop. Antioch. hom.* 22.

Second, we differ from them touching the means of purgation. They say that men are purged by suffering pain in purgatory, whereby they satisfy for their venial sins and for the temporal punishment of their mortal sins. We teach the contrary, holding that nothing can free us from the least punishment of the smallest sin, but the sufferings of Christ—and purge us from the least taint of corruption, saving the blood of Christ. Indeed, they say that our sufferings in themselves considered, do not purge and satisfy, but as they are made meritorious by the sufferings of Christ. But to this I oppose one text of Scripture, where it is said that "Christ hath purged our sins by himself" (Heb. 1:3), where the last clause cuts the throat of all human satisfactions and merits. And it gives us to understand that whatsoever thing purges us from our sins is not to be found in us, but in Christ alone. Otherwise it should have been said that Christ purges the sins of men by themselves, as well as by Himself—and He should merit by His death, that we should become our own saviors in part.

To this place I may well refer prayer for the dead, of which I will propound two conclusions affirmative, and one negative:[8]

Conclusion 1. We hold that Christian charity is to extend itself to the very dead, and it must show itself in their honest burial, in the preservation of their good names, in the help and relief of their posterity, as time and occasion shall be offered [Ruth 1:8; John 19:40].

Conclusion 2. We pray further in general manner for the faithful departed that God would hasten their joyful resurrection and the full accomplishment of their happiness, both for the body and soul. And thus much we ask in saying, "Thy kingdom come," that is, not only the kingdom of grace, but also the kingdom of glory in heaven. Thus far we come, but nearer the gates of Babylon we dare not approach.

8. This paragraph break is not in the original.

Conclusion 3. To pray for particular men departed, and to pray for their deliverance out of purgatory, we think it unlawful, because we have neither promise nor commandment so to do.

THE EIGHTEENTH POINT

Of the Supremacy in Causes Ecclesiastical

I. Our Consent

Touching the point of supremacy ecclesiastical I will set down how near we may come to the Roman Church in two conclusions:[1]

Conclusion 1. For the founding of the primitive church, the ministry of the Word was distinguished by degrees not only of order, but also of power—and Peter was called to the highest degree. Christ "ascended up on high and gave gifts unto men," for the good of His church, "as some to be apostles, some prophets, some evangelists, some pastors and doctors" (Eph. 4:11). Now, howsoever one apostle be not above another, or one evangelist above another, or one pastor above another, yet an apostle was above an evangelist, and an evangelist above all pastors and teachers. And Peter was by calling an apostle, and therefore above all evangelists and pastors, having the highest room in the ministry of the New Testament, both for order and authority.

1. This paragraph break is not in the original.

Conclusion 2. Among the twelve apostles, Peter had a threefold privilege or prerogative: 1. The prerogative of authority. 2. Of primacy. 3. Of principality. For the first, by the privilege of authority, I mean a preeminence in regard of estimation, whereby he was had in reverence above the rest of the twelve apostles; for Cephas, with James and John "are called pillars" and "seemed to be great" (Gal. 2:6, 9). Again, he had the preeminence of primacy because he was the first named, as the foreman of the quest. "The names of the twelve apostles are these, *the first* is Simon, called Peter" (Matt. 10:2). Third, he had the preeminence of principality among the twelve because in regard of the measure of grace, he excelled the rest. For when Christ asked His disciples whom they said He was, Peter, as being of the greatest ability and zeal, answered for them all [Matt. 6:16]. I use this clause, *among the twelve*, because Paul excelled Peter every way—in learning, zeal, understanding—as far as Peter excelled the rest. And thus near we come to popish supremacy.

II. The Difference

The Church of Rome gives to Peter a supremacy under Christ above all causes and persons. That is, full power to govern and order the Catholic Church upon the whole earth, both for doctrine and regiment. This supremacy stands (as they teach) in a power of judgment, to determine of the true sense of all places of Scripture; to determine all causes of faith; to assemble general councils; to ratify the decrees of the said[2] councils; to excommunicate any man upon earth that lives within the church, even princes and nations; properly to absolve and forgive sins; to decide causes brought to him by appeal from all the parts of the earth; lastly, to make laws that shall bind the conscience. This fullness of power with one consent is ascribed to Peter and the bishops of Rome that follow him in a supposed succession. Now we hold on the

2. The 1635 edition omits the word *said.*

contrary, that neither Peter, nor any bishop of Rome, has any supremacy over the catholic church, but that all supremacy under Christ is pertaining to kings and princes within their dominions. And that this our doctrine is good and theirs false and forged, I will make it manifest by sundry reasons:

Reason 1. Christ must be considered of us as a king two ways. First, as He is God; and so is He an absolute king over all things in heaven and earth, with the Father and the Holy Ghost, by the right of creation. Second, He is a king as He is a redeemer of mankind; and by the right of redemption He is a sovereign king over the whole church, and that in special manner. Now as Christ is God with the Father and the Holy Ghost, He has His deputies on earth to govern the world, as namely kings and princes, who are therefore in Scripture called *gods*. But as Christ is Mediator, and consequently a King over His redeemed ones, He has neither fellow nor deputy. No fellow—for then He should be an imperfect mediator. No deputy—for no creature is capable of this office, to do in the room and stead of Christ that which He Himself does. Because every work of the Mediator is a compound work, arising of the effects of two natures concurring in one and the same action, namely the Godhead and the manhood. And therefore, to the effecting of the said work, there is required an infinite power which far exceeds the strength of any created nature. Again [in] Hebrews 7:24, Christ is said to have a priesthood which cannot pass from His person to any other. Whence it follows that neither His kingly nor His prophetical office can pass from Him to any creature—either in whole or in part—because the three offices of mediation in this regard be equal. No, it is a needless thing for Christ to have a deputy to put in execution any part of His mediatorship, considering a deputy only serves to supply the absence of the principal, whereas Christ is always present with His church by His Word and Spirit. For where two or three be gathered together in His name,

He is in the midst among them. It may be said that the ministers in the work of the ministry are deputies of Christ. I answer that they are no deputies, but active instruments. For in the preaching of the Word there be two actions: the first is the uttering or propounding of it to the ear; the second is the inward operation of the Holy Ghost in the heart, which indeed is the principal and belongs to Christ alone, the action of speaking in the minister being only instrumental. Thus likewise, the church of God, in cutting off any member by excommunication, is no more but an instrument performing a ministry in the name of Christ; and that is, to testify and pronounce whom Christ Himself has cut off from the kingdom of heaven—whom He also will have, for this cause, to be severed from the company of His own people until he repents. And so it is in all ecclesiastical actions. Christ has no deputy but only instruments, the whole entire action being personal in respect of Christ. This one conclusion overthrows not only the pope's supremacy, but also many other points of popery.

Reason 2. All the apostles in regard of power and authority were equal, for the commission apostolical both for right and execution was given equally to them all, as the very words import: "Go teach all nations, baptizing them, etc." (Matt. 28:19). And the promise, "I will give to thee the keys of the kingdom of heaven," is not private to Peter, but is made in his person to the rest according as his confession was in the name of the rest. Thus says Theophylact, [on] Mark 16: "They have the power of committing and binding that receive the gift of a bishop as Peter." And Ambrose says, in Psalm 38, "What is said to Peter is said to the apostles." Therefore, Peter had no supremacy over the rest of the apostles in respect of right to the commission, which they say belongs to him only, and the execution thereof to the rest. But let all be granted that Peter was in commission above the rest for the time of his life. Yet hence may not any superiority be gathered for the bishops of Rome because the authority of the apostles was personal, and consequently ceased with them, without being conveyed to any other because the Lord did not vouchsafe the like honor to any after them. For first of all, it was the privilege of the apostles to be called immediately, and to see the Lord Jesus. Second, they had power to give the gift of the Holy Ghost by the imposition of hands. Third, they had such a measure of the assistance of the Spirit, that in their public sermons, and in [the] writing of the Word, they could not err. And these things were all denied to those that followed after them. And that their authority ceased in their persons, it stands with reason also, because it was given in so ample a manner for the founding of the church of the New Testament; which being once founded, it was needful only that there should be pastors and teachers for the building of it up unto the end of the world.

Reason 3. When the sons of Zebedee sued unto Christ for the greatest rooms of honor in His kingdom (deeming He should be an earthly king), Christ answers them again, "Ye know that the Lords of the Gentiles have dominion and they that are great exercise authority over them: but it shall not be so with you." Bernard applies these very words to Pope Eugenius on this manner: "It is plain," says he, "that here dominion is forbidden the apostles. Go to then; dare if you will, to take upon you ruling and apostleship, or in your apostleship rule or dominion; if you will have both alike, you shall lose both. Otherwise you must not think yourself exempted from the number of them of whom the Lord complains thus: they have reigned, but not of me; they have been, and I have not known them."[3]

Reason 4. [Eph. 4:11.] Mention is made of gifts which Christ gave to His church after His ascension, whereby some were apostles,

3. In the margin: *De consider. ad Eug. l.* 2.

some prophets, some evangelists, some pastors and teachers. Now if there had been an office in which men, as deputies of Christ, should have governed the whole church to the end of the world, the calling might here have been named fitly with a gift thereto pertaining. And Paul (no doubt) would not here have concealed it where he mentions callings of lesser importance.

Reason 5. The pope's supremacy was judged by sentences of Scripture and condemned long before it was manifest in the world; the Spirit of prophecy foreseeing and foretelling the state of things to come. "The man of sin (which is that Antichrist) shall exalt himself above all that is called God, etc." (2 Thess. 2:3–4). Now this whole chapter with all the circumstances thereof, most fitly agrees to the see of Rome and the head thereof. And the thing which then stayed the revealing of the man of sin [v. 6], is of the most expounded to be the Roman emperor. I will allege one testimony in the room of many. Chrysostom says on this place, "As long as the empire shall be had in awe, no man shall straightly submit himself to Antichrist; but after that empire shall be dissolved, Antichrist shall invade the estate of the empire standing void, and shall labor to pull unto himself the empire both of man and God." And this we find now in experience to be true, for the see of Rome never flourished until the Empire decayed, and the seat thereof was removed from the city of Rome. Again, [in] Revelation 13, mention is made of two beasts, one coming out of the sea, whom the papists confess to be the heathenish Roman Emperor; the second coming out of the earth, which does all that the first beast could do before him. And this fitly agrees to the popes of Rome, who do and have done all things that the emperor did or could do, and that in his very sight.

Reason 6. The judgment of the ancient church. Cyprian says, "Doubtless the same were the rest of the apostles that Peter was, endued with *equal* fellowship both of honor and of *power*; but a beginning is made of unity that the church may appear to be one."[4] Gregory says, "If one be called universal bishop, the universal church goes to decay."[5] And chapter 144: "I say boldly, that whosoever calls or desires to call himself universal priest, in his pride is a *forerunner of Antichrist*." And, "Behold in the preface of the epistle which you directed unto me, you caused to be set a *proud title*, calling me universal pope."[6] Bernard, "Consider that you are not a lord of bishops, but one of them. Churches are *maimed* in that the Roman bishop draws all power to himself."[7] Again Gregory himself, being pope, says to the emperor, "I which *am subject to your commandment*...have every way discharged that which was due in that I have performed my *allegiance to the emperor*, and have not concealed what I thought on God's behalf." And Pope Leo the Fourth, 200 years after Gregory, acknowledged the Emperor Lotharius for "his sovereign prince" and professed obedience without gainsaying to his imperial commandments.[8]

To conclude, whereas they say that there is a double head of the church, one imperial, which is Christ alone, the other ministerial, which is the pope governing the whole church under Christ; I answer, this distinction robs Christ of His honor because in setting up their ministerial head, they are fain to borrow of Christ things proper unto Him, as the privilege to forgive sins properly and the power to govern the whole earth by making of laws that shall as truly bind conscience as the laws of God, etc.[9]

---

4. In the margin: *De simplicit. praelat.*
5. In the margin: *In registro. l.* 6. *cap.* 118.
6. In the margin: *Lib.* 7. *c.* 30.
7. In the margin: *Ad Eug. lib.* 3.
8. In the margin: *C. de capitulis. dist.* 10.
9. In the margin: Allen's book of priesthood.

THE NINETEENTH POINT

Of the Efficacy of the Sacraments

I. Our Consent

Conclusion 1. We teach and believe that the sacraments are signs to represent Christ with His benefits unto us.

Conclusion 2. We teach further, that the sacraments are indeed instruments whereby God offers and gives the foresaid benefits unto us. Thus far we consent with the Roman Church.

II. The Difference

The difference between us stands in sundry points:[1]

First of all, the best learned among them teach that sacraments are *physical instruments*, that is, true and proper instrumental causes, having force and efficacy in them to produce and give grace.[2] They use to express their meaning by these comparisons: "When the scrivener[3] takes the pen into his hand and writes, the action of writing comes from the pen moved by the hand of the writer. And in cutting of wood or stone, the division comes from the saw moved by

1. This paragraph break is not in the original.
2. In the margin: *Bellar. de Sacram. l. 2. cap.* 11.
3. *Scrivener:* clerk, scribe, or notary.

the hand of the workman. Even so the grace," say they, "that is given by God, is conferred by the sacrament itself." Now we for our parts hold that sacraments are not physical, but mere voluntary instruments. Voluntary, because it is the will and appointment of God to use them as certain outward means of grace. Instruments, because when we use them aright, according to the institution, God then answerably confers grace from Himself. In this respect only take we them for instruments and not otherwise.

The second difference is this: They teach that the very action of the minister dispensing the sacraments—as it is the *work done*—gives grace immediately, if the party be prepared; as the very washing or sprinkling of water in baptism and the giving of bread in the Lord's Supper; even as the orderly moving of the pen upon the paper by the hand of the writer causes writing. We hold the contrary, namely, that no action in the dispensation of a sacrament confers grace as it is a work done, that is, by the efficacy and force of the very sacramental action itself, though ordained of God. But for two other ways: First, by the signification thereof. For God testifies unto us His will and good pleasure partly by the Word of promise and partly by the sacrament; the signs representing to the eyes that which the Word does to the ears, being also types and certain images of the very same things that are promised in the Word and no other. Yes, the elements are not general and confused, but particular signs to the several communicants and by the virtue of the institution. For when the faithful receive the signs from God by the hands of the minister, it is as much as if God Himself—with His own mouth—should speak unto them severally, and by name promise to them remission of sins. And things said to them particularly do more affect, and more take away doubting, than if they were generally spoken to a whole company. Therefore, signs of graces are, as it were, an applying and binding of the promise of salvation to every particular believer. And by this means, the oftener they are received, the more they help our infirmity and confirm our assurance of mercy.

Again, the sacrament confers grace in that the sign thereof confirms faith as a pledge, by reason it has a promise annexed to it. For when God commands us to receive the signs in faith, and withal promises to the receivers to give the thing signified, He binds Himself, as it were, in bond unto us, to stand to His own Word; even as men bind themselves in obligations, putting to their hand and seals so as they cannot go back. And when the signs are thus used as pledges, and that often, they greatly increase the grace of God as a token sent from one friend to another renews and confirms the persuasion of love.

There are the two principal ways whereby the sacraments are said to confer grace, namely, in respect of their signification and as they are pledges of God's favor unto us. And the very point here to be considered is in what order and manner they confirm. And the manner is this: The signs and visible elements affect the senses outwardly and inwardly. The senses convey their object to the mind. The mind, directed by the Holy Ghost, reasons on this manner, out of the promise annexed to the sacrament: He that uses the elements aright shall receive grace thereby. "But I use the elements aright in faith and repentance," says the mind of the believer, "therefore shall I receive from God increase of grace." Thus then, faith is confirmed, not by the work done, but by a kind of reasoning caused in the mind, the argument or proof whereof is borrowed from the elements, being signs and pledges of God's mercy.

The third difference: The papists teach that in the sacrament—by the work done—the very grace of justification is conferred. We say no. Because a man of years must first believe and be justified before he can be a meet partaker of any sacrament. And the grace that is conferred is only the increase of our faith, hope, sanctification, etc.

Our Reasons

Reason 1. The Word preached and the sacraments differ in the manner of giving Christ and His benefits unto us because in the Word the Spirit of God teaches us by a voice conveyed to the mind by the bodily ears; but in the sacraments annexed to the Word by certain sensible and bodily signs viewed by the eye. Sacraments are nothing but visible words and promises.[4] Otherwise, for the giving itself, they differ not. Christ Himself says, that in the very word "is eaten his own flesh, which he was to give for the life of the world" (John 6:51). And what can be said more of the Lord's Supper? Augustine says that "believers are partakers of the body and blood of Christ in baptism."[5] And Jerome to Edibia, that "in baptism we eat and drink the body and blood of Christ." If thus much may be said of baptism, why may it not also be said of the Word preached? Again, Jerome upon Ecclesiastes says, "It is profitable to be filled with the body of Christ, and drink His blood, not only in mystery, but in knowledge of Holy Scripture."[6] Now upon this it follows that seeing the work done in the Word preached confers not grace, neither does the work done in the sacrament confer any grace.

Reason 2. "I baptize you with water to repentance, but he that cometh after me is stronger than I...He shall baptize you with the Holy Ghost and with fire" (Matt. 3:11). Hence it is manifest that grace in the sacrament proceeds not from any action in the sacrament. For John, though he does not disjoin himself and his action from Christ and the action of His Spirit, yet he distinguishes them plainly in number, persons, and effect. To this purpose Paul, who had said of the Galatians that he "travailed of them" and "begat them by the gospel" (Gal. 4:19), says of himself

4. In the margin: *Aug. l.* 19 *contra Faust. cap.* 16.

5. In the margin: *Serm. ad infant. ad altar de Sacr.*

6. In the margin: *Cap.* 3.

that "he is not anything," not only as he was a man but as he was a faithful apostle (1 Cor. 3:7)—thereby excluding the whole evangelical ministry whereof the sacrament is a part, from the least part of divine operation, or efficacy in conferring of grace.

Reason 3. The blessed angels, no, the very flesh of the Son of God, has not any quickening virtue from itself. But all this efficacy or virtue is in and from the Godhead of the Son, who by means of the flesh apprehended by faith, derives heavenly and spiritual life from Himself to the members. Now if there be no efficacy in the flesh of Christ, but by reason of the hypostatical union, how shall bodily actions about bodily elements confer grace immediately?

Reason 4. Paul, [in] Romans 4, stands much upon this to prove that justification by faith is not conferred by the sacraments. And from the circumstance of time he gathers that Abraham was first justified, and then afterward received circumcision, the sign and seal of this righteousness. Now we know that the general condition of all sacraments is one and the same, and that baptism succeeded circumcision. And what can be more plain than the example of Cornelius, [in] Acts 10, who before Peter came unto him, had the commendation of the fear of God, and was endued with the spirit of prayer? And afterward when Peter, by preaching, opened more fully the way of the Lord, he and the rest received the Holy Ghost. And after all this they were baptized. Now if they received the Holy Ghost before baptism, then they received remission of sins and were justified before baptism.

Reason 5. The judgment of the ancient church. Basil [says]: "If there be any grace in the water, it is not from the nature of the water, but from the *presence of the Spirit*."[7] Jerome says, "Man gives water, but God gives the Holy Ghost."[8] Augustine

7. In the margin: *Lib. de Spir. san. cap.* 15.

8. In the margin: *In Esa.* 14.

says, "Water touches the body and washes the heart," but he shows his meaning elsewhere: "There is one water," says he, "of the sacrament; another of the Spirit. The water of the sacrament is visible, the water of the Spirit invisible. That washes the body *and signifies* what is done in the soul; by this the soul is purged and healed."[9]

Objection 1. Remission of sins, regeneration, and salvation are ascribed to the sacrament of baptism [Acts 22:16; Eph. 5:26; Gal. 3:27; Titus 3:5]. *Answer.* Salvation and remission of sins are ascribed to baptism and the Lord's Supper, as to the Word, which is the power of God to salvation to all that believe; and that, as they are instruments of the Holy Ghost to signify, seal, and exhibit to the believing mind the foresaid benefits. But indeed, the proper instrument whereby salvation is apprehended is faith, and sacraments are but props of faith furthering salvation two ways: first, because by their signification they help to nourish and preserve faith; second, because they seal grace and salvation to us. Yes, God gives grace and salvation when we use them well; so be it we believe the Word of promise made to the sacrament, whereof also they are seals. And thus we keep the middle way—neither giving too much nor too little to the sacraments.[10]

---

9. In the margin: *Tract.* 6. *in epist. Ioh.*

10. The 1635 edition says *sacrament.*

THE TWENTIETH POINT

Of Saving Faith; or, the Way to Life

I. Our Consent

Conclusion 1. They teach it to be the property of faith to believe the whole Word of God, and especially the redemption of mankind by Christ.

Conclusion 2. They avouch that they believe and look to be saved by Christ— and by Christ alone—and by the mere mercy of God in Christ.

Conclusion 3. Third, the most learned among them hold and confess that the obedience of Christ is imputed unto them for the satisfaction of the law, and for their reconciliation with God.

Conclusion 4. They avouch that they put their whole trust and confidence in Christ—and in the mere mercy of God—for their salvation.

Conclusion 5. Lastly, they hold that every man must apply the promise of life everlasting by Christ unto himself, and this they grant we are bound to do. And in these five points do they and we agree, at least in show of words.

By the avouching of these five conclusions, papists may easily escape the hands of many magistrates. And unless the mystery of popish doctrine be well known, any common man may easily be deceived and take such for good Protestants that are but popish priests. To this end therefore, that we may the better discern their guile, I will show wherein they fail in each of their conclusions and wherein they differ from us.

II. The Difference

Touching the first conclusion, they believe indeed all the written Word of God, and more than all, for they also believe the books Apocryphal, which antiquity for many hundred years has excluded from the canon. Yes, they believe unwritten traditions received (as they say) from councils, the writings of the fathers, and the determinations of the church, making them also of equal credit with the written Word of God, given by inspiration of the Spirit. Now we for our parts despise not the Apocrypha, as namely, the books of the Maccabees, Ecclesiasticus, and the rest, but we reverence them in all convenient manner, preferring them before any other books of men in that they have been approved by a universal consent of the church. Yet we think them not meet to be received into the canon of Holy Scripture, and therefore not to be believed but as they are consenting with the written Word. And for this our doing we have direction from Athanasius, Origen, Jerome, and the Council of Laodicea. As for unwritten traditions, they come not within the compass of our faith; neither can they, because they come unto us by the hands of men that may deceive and be deceived. And we hold and believe that the right canon of the books of the Old and New Testament contains in it sufficient direction for the church of God to life everlasting, both for faith and manners. Here then is the point of difference, that they make the object of faith larger than it should be or can be. And we keep ourselves to the written Word, believing nothing to salvation out[side] of it.

In the second conclusion, touching salvation by Christ alone, there is a manifest deceit, because they craftily include and couch their own works under the name of Christ. "For," say they, "works done by men regenerate are not their own but Christ's in them. And as they are the works of Christ, they save and no otherwise." But we for our parts look to be saved only by such works as Christ Himself did in His own person, and not by any work at all done by Him in us. For all works done are in the matter of justification and salvation opposed to the grace of Christ. "Election is of grace, not of works; if it be of works it is no more of grace" (Rom. 11:6). Again, whereas they teach that we are saved by the works of Christ which He works in us, and makes us to work; it is flat against the Word. For Paul says, "We are not saved by such works as God hath ordained that men regenerate should walk in" (Eph. 2:10). And he says further, "that he counted *all things*," even after his conversion, "loss unto him, that he might be found in Christ, not having his own righteousness which is of the law" (Phil. 3:8). Again, "Christ washed away our sins by himself" (Heb. 1:3), which last words exclude the merit of all works done by Christ within man. Thus indeed, the papists overturn all that which in word they seem to hold touching their justification and salvation. We confess with them, that good works in us are the works of Christ, yet are they not Christ's alone, but ours also in that they proceed from Christ by the mind and will of man, as water from the fountain by the channel. And look, as the channel defiled defiles the water that is without defilement in the fountain, even so the mind and will of man defiled by the remnants of sin defile the works, which—as they come from Christ—are undefiled. Hence it is that the works of grace which we do by Christ—or Christ in us—are defective and must be severed from Christ in the act of justification or salvation.

The third conclusion is touching the imputation of Christ's obedience, which some of the most learned among them acknowledge, and the difference between us stands on this manner: They hold that Christ's obedience is imputed only to make satisfaction for sin and not to justify us before God. We hold and believe that the obedience of Christ is imputed to us even for our righteousness before God. Paul says, "Christ is made unto us of God, wisdom, *righteousness, sanctification*, and redemption" (1 Cor. 1:30). Hence, I reason thus: "If Christ be both our sanctification and our righteousness, then He is not only unto us inherent righteousness but also righteousness imputed. But He is not only our sanctification (which the papists themselves expound of inherent or habitual righteousness) but also our righteousness; for thus by Paul are they distinguished. Therefore, He is unto us both inherent and imputed righteousness." And very reason teaches us thus much. For in the end of the world, at the bar of God's judgment, we must bring some kind of righteousness for our justification that may stand in the rigor of the law according to which we are to be judged. But our inherent righteousness is imperfect, and stained with manifold defects, and shall be as long as we live in this world, as experience tells us. And consequently, it is not suitable to the justice of the law. And if we go out of ourselves, we shall find no righteousness serving for our turns either in men or angels that may or can procure our absolution before God and acceptation to life everlasting. We must therefore have recourse to the Person of Christ—and His obedience imputed unto us must serve not only to be a satisfaction to God for all our sins but also for our perfect justification, in that God is content to accept of it for our righteousness as if it were inherent in us or performed by us.

Touching the fourth conclusion, they hold it the safest and surest course to put their trust and confidence in the mercy of God alone for their salvation. Yet they condescend that men may also put their confidence in the merit of their own works and in the merits also of other men, so it be in sobriety.[1] But this doctrine quite mars the conclusion, because, by teaching that men are to put confidence in the creature, they overturn all confidence in the Creator. For in the very first commandment we are taught to make choice of the true God for our God, which thing we do when we give to God our hearts. And we give our hearts to God when we put our whole confidence in Him for the salvation of our souls. Now then, to put confidence in men or in works is to make them our gods. The true and ancient form of making confession was on this manner: "I believe in God the Father, in Jesus Christ, and in the Holy Ghost," without mention making of any confidence in works or creatures. The ancient church never knew any such confession or confidence. Cyprian says, "He believes not in God who puts not affiance[2] concerning his salvation in God alone."[3] And indeed the papists themselves, when death comes, forsake the confidence of their merits and fly to the mere mercy of God in Christ. And for a confirmation of this, I allege the testimony of one Ulinbergius of Colen who writes thus: "There was a book found in the vestry of a certain parish of Colen, written in the Dutch tongue, in the year of our Lord, 1475, which the priests used in visiting the sick.[4] And in it these questions be found. 'Do you believe that you cannot be saved but by the death of Christ?' The sick person answered, 'Yes.' Then it is said unto him, 'Go to then while breath remains in you, put your confidence in this *death alone*; have affiance in nothing else; commit yourself wholly to this death; with it alone cover yourself; dive yourself in every part into this death;

1. In the margin: *Bellar. l.* 5. *c.* 7. *de iustific.*

2. *Affiance*: trust.

3. In the margin: *De duplici Martyr.*

4. In the margin: *Lib. de causis cur Evang. p.* 436.

in every part pierce yourself with it; enfold yourself in this death. And if the Lord will judge you, say, 'Lord, I put the death of our Lord Jesus Christ between me and your judgment, and by *no other means* I contend with you.' And if He shall say unto you, that you are a sinner; say: 'Lord, the death of my Lord Jesus Christ, I put between you and my sins.' If He shall say unto you, that you have deserved damnation, say, 'Lord, I oppose the death of our Lord Jesus Christ between you and my evil merits, and I *offer His merit for the merit which I should have, and have not.*' If He shall say that He is angry with you, say, 'Lord, I oppose the death of our Lord Jesus Christ between me and your anger.'"[5] Here we see what papists do and have done in the time of death. And that which they hold and practice, when they are dying, they should hold and practice every day while they are living.

In the last conclusion, they teach that we must not only believe in general, but also apply unto ourselves the promises of life everlasting. But they differ from us in the very manner of applying. They teach that the promise is to be applied, not by faith assuring us of our own salvation, but only by hope, in likelihood conjectural. We hold that we are bound in duty to apply the promise of life by faith without making doubt thereof, and by hope to continue the certainty after the apprehension made by faith. We do not teach that all and every man living within the precincts of the church—professing the name of Christ—is certain of his salvation, and that by faith, but that he ought so to be, and must endeavor to attain thereto. And here is a great point in the mystery of iniquity to be considered. For by this uncertain application of the promise of salvation, and this wavering hope, they overturn half the doctrine of the gospel. For it enjoins two things: first, to believe the

---

5. In the margin: Supposed to be questions of Anselm.

promises thereof to be true in themselves; second, to believe, and by faith to apply them unto ourselves. And this latter part, without which the former is void of comfort, is quite overturned. The reasons which they allege against our doctrine I have answered before; now therefore I let them pass.

To conclude, though in colored terms they seem to agree with us in doctrine concerning faith, yet indeed they deny and abolish the substance thereof, namely, the particular and certain application of Christ crucified and His benefits unto ourselves. Again, they fail in that they cut off the principal duty and office of true saving faith, which is, to apprehend and to apply the blessing promised.

THE TWENTY-FIRST POINT

Of Repentance

I. Our Consent

Conclusion 1. That repentance is the conversion of a sinner. There is a twofold conversion: passive and active. Passive is an action of God, whereby He converts man, being as yet unconverted. Active is an action whereby man, being once turned of God, turns himself; and of the latter must this conclusion be understood. For the first conversion, considering it is a work of God turning us unto Himself, is not the repentance whereof the Scripture speaks so oft, but it is called by the name of regeneration; and repentance, whereby we, being first turned of God, do turn ourselves, and do good works, is the fruit thereof.

Conclusion 2. That repentance stands especially for practice, in contrition of heart, confession of mouth, and satisfaction in work or deed. Touching contrition, there be two kinds thereof: legal and evangelical. Legal contrition is nothing but a remorse of conscience for sin in regard of the wrath and judgment of God, and it is no grace of God at all; nor any part, or cause of repentance, but only an occasion thereof, and that by the mercy of God. For of itself, it is the sting of the law, and the very entrance into the pit of hell. Evangelical contrition is when a repentant sinner is grieved for his sins—not so much for fear of hell or any other punishment, as because he has offended and displeased so good and merciful a God. This contrition is caused by the ministry of the gospel, and in the practice of repentance it is always necessary and goes before as the beginning thereof. Second, we hold and maintain that confession is to be made and that in sundry respects: first to God, both publicly in the congregation and also privately in our secret and private prayers. Second to the church, when any person has openly offended the congregation by any crime and is therefore excommunicate. Third, to our private neighbor, when we have upon any occasion offended and wronged him. "If thou bring thy gift to the altar, and there rememberest that thy brother hath ought against thee, go first and be reconciled to him" (Matt. 5:23). Now reconciliation presupposes confession. Lastly, in all true repentance, we hold and acknowledge there must be satisfaction made: First to God, and that is when we entreat Him in our supplications to accept the death and passion of Christ, as a full, perfect, and sufficient satisfaction for all our sins. Second, it is to be made unto the church, after excommunication for the public offences; and it stands in duties of humiliation that fitly serve to testify the truth of our repentance. Third, satisfaction is to be made to our neighbor. Because if he be wronged, he must have recompense and restitution made [Luke 29:8]; and there repentance may justly be suspected, where no satisfaction is made, if it lie in our power.

Conclusion 3. That in repentance we are to bring forth outward fruits worthy [of] amendment of life. For repentance itself is in the heart, and therefore must be testified in all manner of good works, whereof the principal is, to endeavor day by day—by God's grace—to leave and renounce all and every sin, and in all things to do the will of God. And here let it be remembered that we are not patrons of licentiousness and enemies of good works. For though we exclude them from the act of our justification and salvation, yet we maintain a profitable and necessary use of them in the life of every Christian man. This use is threefold: in respect of God, of man, of ourselves. Works are to be done in respect of God that His commandments may be obeyed [1 John 3:22], that His will may be done [1 Thess. 4:3], that we may show ourselves to be obedient children to God our Father [1 Peter 1:14], that we may show ourselves thankful for our redemption by Christ [Titus 2:14], that we might not grieve the Spirit of God [Eph. 4:30], but walk according to the same [Gal. 5:22],[1] that God by our good works may be glorified [Matt. 5:16], that we may be good followers of God [Eph. 5:1]. Again, works are to be done in regard of men, that our neighbor may be helped in worldly things [Luke 6:38], that he may be won by our example to godliness [1 Peter 3:14], that we may prevent in ourselves the giving of any offence [1 Cor. 10:32], that by doing good we may stop the mouths of our adversaries. Third and lastly, they have use in respect of ourselves, that we may show ourselves to be new creatures [2 Cor. 5:17], that we may walk as the children of light [Eph. 5:8], that we have some assurance of our faith, and of our salvation [2 Peter 1:8, 10], that we may discern dead and counterfeit faith from true faith [James 2:17], that faith and the gifts of God may be exercised and continued unto the end [2 Tim. 1:6], that the punishments of sin, both temporal and eternal, may be prevented [Ps. 89:32], that the reward may be obtained, which God freely in mercy has promised to men for their good works [Gal. 6:9].

---

1. The 1635 edition incorrectly indicates: *Gal. 6:22*.

II. The Difference

We dissent not from the Church of Rome in the doctrine of repentance itself, but in the damnable abuses thereof; which are of two sorts: general and special.[2]

General [abuses] are those which concern repentance wholly considered; and they are these: The *first*, is that they place the beginning of repentance [partly in themselves and][3] partly in the Holy Ghost, or in the power of their natural freewill, being helped by the Holy Ghost; whereas Paul indeed ascribes this work wholly unto God: "Proving if God at any time will give them repentance" (2 Tim. 2:25).[4] And men that are not weak, but dead in trespasses and sins, cannot do anything that may further their conversion, though they be helped never so much; no more than dead men in their graves can rise from thence. The *second* abuse is that they take penance, or rather repentance, for that public discipline and order of correction that was used against notorious offenders in the open congregation. For the Scripture sets down but one repentance, and that common to all men without exception, and to be practiced in every part of our lives for the necessary mortification of sin; whereas open ecclesiastical correction pertained not to all and every man within the compass of the church, but to them alone that gave any open offence. The *third* abuse is that they make repentance to be not only a virtue but also a sacrament; whereas for the space of a thousand years after Christ, and upward, it was not reckoned among the sacraments. Yes, it seems that Lombard was one of the first that called it a sacrament; and the schoolmen after him disputed of the matter and form of this sacrament, not able any of them certainly to define what should be the outward element. The *fourth* abuse is

2. This paragraph break is not in the original.

3. The 1635 edition does not include the words *partly in themselves and.*

4. The 1635 edition incorrectly indicates: *1 Tim. 2:25.*

touching the effect and efficacy of repentance, for they make it a meritorious cause of remission of sins and of life everlasting, flat against the Word of God. Paul says notably, "we are justified freely by his grace through the redemption which is in Christ Jesus, whom God hath sent to be a reconciliation by faith in his blood" (Rom. 3:24–25). In these words, these forms of speech, "redemption in Christ," "reconciliation in his blood by faith," [and] "freely by grace," must be observed and considered. For they show plainly that no part of satisfaction or redemption is wrought in us or by us, but out of us only in the Person of Christ. And therefore, we esteem of repentance only as a fruit of faith, and the effect—or efficacy of it—is to testify remission of our sins and our reconciliation before God. It will be said that, "Remission of sins and life everlasting are promised to repentance." *Answer.* It is not to the work of repentance but the person which repents; and that not for his own merits or work of repentance, but for the merits of Christ, which he applies to himself by faith. And thus are we to understand the promises of the gospel, in which works are mentioned, presupposing always in them the reconciliation of the person with God, to whom the promise is made. Thus we see wherefore we dissent from the Roman Church touching the doctrine of repentance.

Special abuses do concern contrition, confession, and satisfaction. The first abuse, concerning contrition, is that they teach it must be sufficient and perfect. They use now to help the matter by a distinction, saying that the sorrow in contrition must be in the highest degree in respect of value and estimation.[5] Yet the opinion of Adrian was otherwise, that in true repentance a man should be grieved according to all his endeavor.[6] And the Roman Catechism says as much, that "The sorrow conceived of our sins

5. In the margin: *Appretiative non intensive.*

6. In the margin: *q.* 1 *de poenit art.* 2 & *quodlib.* 5. *art.* 3.

must be so great, that *none can be conceived to be greater*; that we must be contrite in the same manner we love God, and that is, with all our heart and strength, in a most *vehement sorrow*; and that the hatred of sin must be not only the greatest, but also *most vehement* and perfect, so as it may exclude all sloth and slackness."[7] Indeed afterward it follows that true contrition may be effectual though it be imperfect. But how can this stand if they will not only commend but also prescribe and avouch that contrition must be most perfect and vehement? We therefore only teach that God requires not so much the measure as the truth of any grace, and that it is a degree of unfeigned contrition to be grieved because we cannot be grieved for our sins as we should. The second abuse is that they ascribe to their contrition the merit of congruity. But this cannot stand with the all-sufficient merit of Christ. And an ancient council says, "*God* inspires into us first of all the faith and love of Himself, *no merits going before*, that we may faithfully require the sacrament of baptism, and after baptism do the things that please Him." And we for our parts hold that God requires contrition at our hands, not to merit remission of sins, but that we may acknowledge our own unworthiness, and be humbled in the sight of God, and distrust all our own merits; and further, that we may make the more account of the benefits of Christ, whereby we are received into the favor of God. Lastly, that we might more carefully avoid all sins in time to come, whereby so many pains and terrors of conscience are procured. And we acknowledge no contrition at all to be meritorious, save that of Christ, whereby He was broken for our iniquities. The third abuse is that they make imperfect contrition, or attrition arising of the fear of hell, to be good and profitable. And to it they apply the saying of the prophet, "The fear of God is the

---

7. In the margin: *cap. de Sacr poenit.*

beginning of wisdom." But servile fear of itself is the fruit of the law, which is the ministry of death and condemnation. And consequently, it is the way to eternal destruction if God leaves men to themselves. And if it turns to the good of any, it is only by accident, because God in mercy makes it to be an occasion going before, of grace to be given. Otherwise remorse of conscience for sin is no beginning of repentance, or the restrainment of any sin; but rather is, and that properly, the beginning of unspeakable horrors of conscience, and everlasting death, unless God show mercy. And yet this fear of punishment, if it be tempered and delayed with other graces and gifts of God in holy men, it is not unprofitable; in whom there is not only a sorrow for punishment, but also, and that much more, for the offence. And such a kind of fear, or sorrow, is commanded: "If I be a father, where is my honor? If I be a Lord, where is my fear?" (Mal. 1:6). And Chrysostom says, that, "The fear of hell in the heart of a just man, is a strong man armed against thieves and robbers to drive them from the house." And Ambrose says that "Martyrs in the time of their sufferings, confirmed themselves against the cruelty of persecutors by setting the fear of hell before their eyes."

Abuses touching confession are these. The first is that they use a form of confession of their sins unto God, uttered in an unknown language; being therefore foolish and ridiculous, withal requiring the aid and intercession of dead men and such as be absent. Whereas, there is but one Mediator between God and man, the man Jesus Christ. The second is that they in practice make confession of their sins not only to God, but to the saints departed, in that they make prayer to them in which they ask their intercession for the pardon of their sins. And this is, not only to match them with God in seeing and knowing the heart, but also to give a part of His divine worship unto them. The third and principal abuse is that they have corrupted canonical confession by turning it into private auricular confession, binding all men in conscience by a law made to confess all their mortal sins, with all circumstances that change the kind of the sin (as far as possibly they can remember) once every year at the least, and that to a priest, unless it be in the case of extreme necessity. But in the Word of God there is no warrant for this confession, nor in the writings of *orthodox* antiquity for the space of many hundred years after Christ, as one of their own side avouches.[8] And the commandment of the Holy Ghost, "Confess one to another and pray one for another" (James 5:16), binds as well the priest to make confession unto us, as any of us to the priest. And whereas it is said, that "many were baptized confessing their sins" (Matt. 3:6), and "many that believed came and confessed and showed their works" (Acts 19:18), the confession was voluntary and not constrained. It was also general and not particular of all and every sin, with the necessary circumstances thereof. And in this liberty of confession the church remained 1,200 years until the Council of Lateran, in which the law of auricular confession was first enacted, being a notable invention serving to discover the secrets of men and to enrich that covetous and ambitious see with the revenues of the world. It was not known to Augustine when he said, "What have I to do with men that they should hear my confessions, as though they should heal all my diseases?"[9] Nor to Chrysostom, when he says, "I do not compel you to confess your sins to others."[10] And, "If you be ashamed to confess them to any man, because you have sinned, say them daily in your own mind. I do not bid you confess them to your fellow servant that he should mock you. Confess them to God that cures you."[11]

---

8. In the margin: *Beatus Rhenatus on Tertul lib. de poenit.*

9. In the margin: *Confess. lib.* 10 *c.* 3.

10. In the margin: *De Deinat hom.* 5. *tom.* 5.

11. In the margin: *Hom.* 2. *in Psalm* 50.

The abuse of satisfaction is that they have turned canonical satisfaction, which was made to the congregation by open offenders, into a satisfaction of the justice of God for the temporal punishment of their sins. Behold here a most horrible profanation of the whole gospel, and especially of the satisfaction of Christ, which of itself without any supply is sufficient every way for the remission both of fault and punishment. But of this point I have spoken before.

Hitherto I have handled and proved by induction of sundry particulars that we are to make a separation from the present Church of Rome in respect of the foundation and substance of true religion. Many more things might be added to this very purpose, but here I conclude this first point, adding only this one caveat, that we make separation from the Roman religion without hatred of the persons that are maintainers of it. No, we join in affection more with them than they with us. They die with us not for their religion (though they deserve it) but for the treasons which they intend and enterprise [Deut. 13:5]. We are ready to do the duties of love unto them enjoined us in the Word. We reverence the good gifts in many of them; we pray for them, wishing their repentance and eternal salvation.

Now I mean to proceed and to touch briefly [on] other points of doctrine contained in this portion of Scripture which I have now in hand. In the second place therefore, out of this commandment, "Go out of her, my people," I gather that the true church of God is and has been in the present Roman church as corn in the heap of chaff. Though popery reigned and overspread the face of the earth for many hundred years, yet in the midst thereof, God reserved a people unto Himself that truly worshipped Him. And to this effect, the Holy Ghost says that the dragon, which is the devil, caused the woman, that is, the church, to flee into the wilderness, where he sought to destroy her but could not. "And she still retains *a remnant of her seed,* which keep the commandments of God and have the testimony of Jesus Christ" (Rev. 12:17). Now this which I speak of the Church of Rome, cannot be said in like manner of the congregations of Turks and other infidels, that the hidden church of God is preserved among them; because there is no means of salvation at all; whereas the Church of Rome has the Scriptures, though in a strange language—and baptism for the outward form—which helps God in all ages preserved, that His elect might be gathered out of the midst of Babylon. This serves to stop the mouths of papists, which demand of us where our church was fourscore years ago, before the days of Luther; whereby they would insinuate to the world that our church and religion is green or new. But they are answered out of this very text, that our church has ever been since the days of the apostles, and that in the very midst of the papacy. It has been always a church and did not first begin to be in Luther's time, but only then began to show itself, as having been hidden by a universal apostasy for many hundred years together. Again, we have here occasion to consider the dealing of God with His own church and people. He will not have them for external society to be mixed with their enemies, and that for special purpose; namely, to exercise the humility and patience of His few servants. When Elijah saw idolatry spread over all Israel, he went apart into the wilderness and in grief desired to die [1 Kings 19:4]. And David cried out, "Woe is me that I am constrained to dwell in Mesheck and to have my habitation in the tents of Kedar" (Ps. 120:5). And just Lot must have his righteous soul vexed with seeing and hearing the abominations of Sodom.

Third, by this commandment we are taught what opinion to carry of the present Church of Rome. It is often demanded whether it be a church or no; and the answer may hence be formed on this manner: If by this church be understood a state or regiment of the people, whereof the pope is head, and the members are all such as do acknowledge him to be their head, and do believe the doctrine established in the Council of Trent, we take it to be no church of God. Because Babylon, which I have proved to be the Church of Rome, is here opposed to the church or people of God; and because we are commanded to come out of it, whereas we may not wholly forsake any people until they forsake Christ. Some will haply[12] say, "The Church of Rome has the Scriptures and the sacrament of baptism." I answer first of all, they have indeed the books of Holy Scripture among them; but by the rest of their doctrine they overthrow the true sense thereof in the foundation, as I have proved before. And though they have the outward form of baptism, yet they overturn the inward baptism, which is the substance of all, standing in the justification and sanctification of a sinner. Again, I answer that they have the Word and baptism, not for themselves, but for the true church of God among them—like as the lantern holds the candle, not for itself, but for others. Second, it may be—and is alleged—that if the pope be Antichrist, he then sits in the temple—that is, the church of God—and by this means the Roman church shall be the true church [2 Thess. 2:4]. *Answer.* He sits in the temple of God, but mark further how: *as God*, that is, not as a member, but as a manifest usurper; like as the thief sits in the true man's house. For the popish church and God's church are mingled like chaff and corn in one heap. And the Church of Rome may be said to be in the church of God, and the church of God in the Church of Rome; as we say the wheat is among the chaff and the chaff in the wheat. Again, he is said to sit in the temple of God, because the Roman church, though falsely, takes unto itself the title of the true catholic church. Some go about to delay

12. *Haply*: by chance.

and qualify the matter, by comparing this church to a man lying sick full of sores, having also his throat cut, yet so as body and soul are joined together, and life is remaining still. But all things well considered, it is rather like a dead carcass, and is void of all spiritual life, as the popish errors in the foundation do manifest. Indeed, a known harlot may afterward remain a wife and be so termed: yet after the bill of divorcement is given, she ceases to be a wife though she can show her marriage ring. Now the church has received the bill of her divorcement in the written Word, namely [in] 2 Thessalonians 2 and Revelation 13:11–12, etc.

Furthermore, in this commandment we may see a lively portraiture of the state of all mankind. Here we see two sorts of men: some are pertaining to Babylon, a people running on to their destruction; some again are a people of God severed from Babylon and reserved to life everlasting. If any ask the cause of this distinction, I answer, "It is the very will of God vouchsafing mercy to some, and forsaking others by withdrawing His mercy from them for the better declaration of His justice." Thus says the Lord, "I have reserved seven thousand that never bowed the knee to Baal" (Rom. 11:4). And the prophet Isaiah says, "Unless the Lord had reserved a remnant, we had been as Sodom and Gomorrah" (Isa. 1:9). By this distinction, we are taught above all things to seek to be of the number of God's people and to labor for assurance of this in our own consciences. For if all should be saved, less care would suffice. But this mercy is not common to all, and therefore the more to be thought upon.

Lastly, here I note the special care that God has over His own children. He first gives them warning to depart before He begins to execute His judgment upon His enemies with whom they live—that they might not be partakers of their sins or punishments. Thus, before God would punish Jerusalem, an angel is sent to mark them in the forehead that mourned for the abominations of the people [Ezek. 9:4]. And in the destruction of the firstborn of Egypt, the angel passed over the houses of the Jews that had their posts sprinkled with the blood of the paschal lamb [Ex. 12:23]. And this passing over betokens safety and preservation in the common destruction, to those that have their hearts sprinkled with the blood of Christ. This blessing of protection should move us all to become true and hearty servants of God. Men usually become members of those societies and corporations where they may enjoy many freedoms and privileges. Well, behold, in the society of the saints of God, which is the true church, there is the freedom from danger in all common destructions, and from eternal vengeance at the last day. When Esther had procured safety for the Jews, and liberty to revenge themselves upon their enemies, it is said that many of the people of the land *became Jews*. Even so, considering Christ has procured freedom from hell, death, and damnation for all that believe in Him, we should labor above all things to become new creatures, enjoining ourselves always to the true church of God.

Hitherto I have spoken of the commandment. Now follows the reason thereof drawn from the end: "that they be not partakers of her sins: and that they receive not of her plagues." Here I might stand long to show what be the sins of the Church of Rome, but I will only name the principal [sins].[13]

The first sin is *atheism*, and that I prove on this manner. Atheism is twofold: open, [and] colored. Open atheism is when men, both in word and deed, deny God and His Word. Colored atheism is not so manifest, and it has two degrees: The first is when men acknowledge God the Creator and Governor of heaven and earth, and yet deny the Father, Son, and Holy Ghost. Thus

13. In the margin: Sins of the Church of Rome.

the Ephesians, before they received the gospel, are said to be *without God*, whom in their natural judgment they acknowledged [Eph. 2:12]—because they denied Christ and consequently worshipped an idol of their own brain in that they worshipped God out of Christ. And in this respect, though the Samaritans worshipped the God of Abraham, yet our Savior Christ says, "they worshipped they knew not what" (John 4:22). And the psalmist says of the Gentiles that "their gods are idols" (Ps. 96:5). In this degree of atheism are placed Turks and Jews at this day, the anti-Trinitarians and Arians, and all that conceive and worship God out of the Trinity. The second degree is, when men do rightly acknowledge the unity of the Godhead in the Trinity of persons, yet so, as by other necessary consequents partly of their doctrine and partly of the service of God, they overturn that which they have well maintained. And thus I say, that the very religion of the Church of Rome is a kind of atheism. For whereas it makes the merit of the works of men to concur with the grace of God, it overthrows the grace of God [Romans 11]. In word they acknowledge the infinite justice and mercy of God, but by consequent both are denied. How can that be infinite justice, which may any way be appeased by human satisfaction? And how shall God's mercy be infinite when we—by our own satisfactions—must add a supply to the satisfaction of Christ? Again, "He that hath not the Son, hath not the Father" (1 John 2:23). And he that has neither Father nor Son, denies God.[14]

Now the present Roman religion has not the Son—that is, Jesus Christ, God and man, the Mediator of mankind—but has transformed Him into a feigned Christ. And I show it thus: For one, Jesus Christ, in all things like unto us in His humanity, sin only excepted, they have framed a Christ to whom they ascribe

14. This paragraph break is not the original.

two kinds of existing: one natural, whereby He is visible, touchable, and circumscribed in heaven; the other not only above but also against nature; by which He is substantially—according to His flesh, in the hands of every priest, in every host, and in the mouth of every communicant—invisible, untouchable, uncircumscribed. And thus, in effect, they abolish His manhood. Yes, they disgrade[15] Him of His offices. For one Jesus Christ, the only King, Lawgiver, and Head of the church, they join unto Him the pope; not only as a vicar, but also as a fellow, in that they give unto him power to make laws binding conscience, to resolve and determine infallibly the sense of Holy Scripture, properly to pardon sin both in respect of fault and temporal punishment, to have authority over the whole earth and a part of hell, to depose kings, to whom under Christ every soul is to be subject, [and] to absolve subjects from the oath of allegiance, etc. For one Jesus Christ, the only real priest of the New Testament, they enjoin many secondary priests unto Him, which offer Christ daily in the mass for the sins of the quick and the dead. For one Jesus Christ, the all-sufficient Mediator of intercession, they have added many fellows unto Him to make request for us, namely, as many saints as be in the pope's calendar. Lastly, for the only merits of Christ, in whom alone the Father is well pleased, they have devised a treasury of the church, containing—beside the merits of Christ—the surplus of the merits of saints, to be dispensed to men at the discretion of the pope. And thus we see that Christ, and consequently God Himself to be worshipped in Christ, is transformed into a fantasy or idol of man's conceit. Again, there is always a proportion between the worship of God and our persuasion of Him. And men, in giving unto God any worship, have respect to His nature, that both may be suitable, and He well-pleased. Let us then see

15. *Disgrade*: to depose of rank or dignity.

what manner of worship the Roman religion affords: It is for the greatest part mere will-worship, without any allowance or commandment from God, as Durand in his *Rationale* in effect acknowledges. It is a carnal service standing of innumerable bodily rites and ceremonies, borrowed partly from the Jews and partly from the heathen. It is divided between God and some of His creatures, in that they are worshipped both with one kind of worship, let them paint it as they can. Thus then, if by their manner of worshipping God, we may judge how they conceive of Him— as we may—they have plainly turned the true God into a fantasy of their own. For God is no otherwise to be conceived than He has revealed Himself in His creatures and Word—and especially in Christ, who is the graven image of the Person of the Father.

The second sin is *idolatry,* and that as gross as was ever among the heathen. And it is to be seen in two things: First, that they worship the saints with religious worship, which without exception is proper to God. Yes, they transform some of them into detestable idols, making them in truth mediators of redemption, especially the virgin Mary, whom they call "a Lady, a Goddess, a Queen, whom Christ her Son obeys in heaven, a mediatress: or life, hope, the medicine of the diseased."[16] And they pray unto her thus, "Prepare you glory for us: defend us from our enemies, and in the hour of death receive us, loose the bonds of the guilty, bring light to the blind, drive away all devils. Show yourself to be a mother. Let Him receive your prayers." Again, their idolatry is manifest, in that they worship God in, at, or before images; having no commandment so to do, but the contrary. They allege that they use and worship images only in a remembrance of God. But this is all one as if an unchaste wife should receive many lovers into her house in the absence of her husband and, being reproved,

16. In the margin: *Bellar. l.* 1. *de sanct. c.* 16. *Missuli* & *Breviario refor.*

should answer that they were the friends of her husband and that she kept them only in remembrance of him. Third, their idolatry exceeds the idolatry of the heathen, in that they worship a breaden god, or Christ in and under the forms of bread and wine. And if Christ according to His humanity be absent from the earth, as I have proved, the popish host is as abominable an idol as ever was.

The third sin is the maintenance of *adultery*. And that is manifest: first of all, in the toleration of the stewes,[17] flat against the commandment of God. "There shall be no whore of the daughters of Israel, neither shall there be a whore keeper of the sons of Israel" (Deut. 23:17). And this toleration is an occasion of uncleanness to many young men and women that otherwise would abstain from all such kind of filthiness. And what an abomination is this, when brother and brother, father and son, nephew and uncle, shall come to one and the same harlot, one before or after the other? Second, their law beyond the fourth degree allows the marriage of any persons; and by this means they sometime allow incest.[18] For in the unequal collateral line, the person next the common stock is a father or mother to the brother's or sister's posterity, as for example:

1. John
   Anne
   Nicholas
2. Thomas
3. Lewis
4. Roger
5. Anthony
6. James

Here Anne and Nicholas are brother and sister, and Anne is distant from James six degrees, he being her nephew afar off. And

17. *Stewes*: brothels.

18. In the margin: *Greg. cap.* 9. *de consang.*

the marriage between them is allowed by the Church of Rome, they not being within the compass of four degrees, which nevertheless is against the law of nature. For Anne, being the sister of Nicholas, is instead of a mother to all that are begotten of Nicholas, even to James, and James's posterity. Yet thus much I grant, that the daughter of Anne may lawfully marry James or Anthony, the case being altered, because they are not one to another as parents and children.

The fourth sin is *magic*, *sorcery*, or *witchcraft*, in the consecration of the host in which they make their breaden god; in exorcisms over holy bread, holy water, and salt; in the casting out or driving away of devils, by the sign of the cross, by solemn conjurations, by holy water, by the ringing of bells, by lighting tapers, by relics, and such like.[19] For these things have not their supposed force either by creation or by any institution of God in His Holy Word; and therefore if anything be done by them, it is from the secret operation of the devil himself.

The fifth sin is that in their doctrine they maintain *perjury*, because they teach with one consent that a papist examined may answer doubtfully against the dire intention of the examiner, framing another meaning unto himself in the ambiguity of his words.[20] As for example, when a man is asked whether he said or heard mass in such a place. Though he did, they affirm he may say no, and swear unto it, because he was not there to reveal it to the examiner. Whereas in the very law of nature, he that takes an oath should swear according to the intention of him that has power to minister an oath; and that in truth, justice, judgment. Let them clear their doctrine from all defense of perjury if they can.

---

19. In the margin: *Mola. Tract.* 2. *cap.* 4. *can.* 3.

20. In the margin: *Mola. Tract.* 2. *c.* 7. *con.* 1. *prop* 6 *idem communiter omnes.*

The sixth sin is, that they *reverse many of God's commandments*, making no sin [that] which God's Word makes a sin. Thus they teach, "that if any man steal some little thing that is thought not to cause any notable hurt, it is no mortal sin"; that, "the officious lie, and the lie made in sport, are venial sins"; that, "to pray for our enemies in particular, is no precept, but a counsel, and that none is bound to salute his enemy in the way of friendship,"[21] flat against the rule of Christ in Matthew 5:47, where the word ἀσπάσησθε signifies all manner of duty and courtesy. That, "rash judgment, though consent come thereto, is regularly but a venial sin." That, "it is lawful otherwise to fain holiness." That, "the painting of the face is ordinarily but a venial sin." That, "it is not lawful to forbid begging," whereas the Lord forbad there should be any beggar in Israel [Deuteronomy 15]. Again, they teach that men in their choler, when they are chiding and swear, *wounds and blood*, are not indeed blasphemers.[22]

Lastly, their writers use manifest *lying* to justify their doctrine. They plead falsely that all antiquity is on their side, whereas it is as much against them as for them; and as much for us as them. Again, their manner has been and is still to prove their opinions, by forged and counterfeit writings of men, some whereof I will name:

1. *Saint James's Liturgy.*
2. *The Canons of the Apostles.*
3. *The books of Dionysius Areopagita*, and namely, *De Hierarchia Ecclesiastica.*
4. *The Decretal Epistles of the Popes.*
5. Pope Clement's *Works.*
6. Some of the *epistles of Ignatius.*

21. In the margin: *Mola. tract.* 2 *ca.* 6. *con.* 1. *prop.* 15. *idem caeteri.*

22. In the margin: *Greg. de Val. tom.* 3. *dis.* 1. *q.* 13 *and Caietan.*

7. Origen's *book of repentance.* His homilies *in diversos sanctos*, *Commentaries on Job*, and *Book of Lamentation.*
8. Chrysostom's *Liturgy.*
9. Basil's *Liturgy* and his *Ascetica.*
10. Augustine's *book de 8 quest. Dulcitii, A Book of True and False Repentance, Serm. de secto commemorationis animarum, Book de dogm., Ecclesiast. Serm. ad fratres in Hereom., Ser. of Peter's Chair, Book of Visiting the Sick, etc.*
11. Justin Martyr's *Questions and Answers.*
12. Athanasius's *Epistle to Pope Felix.*
13. Bernard's *Sermons of the Lord's Supper.*
14. Jerome's *epistle ad Demetriadem favoring of Pelagius.*
15. Tertullian's *de Monogamia.*
16. Cyprian's *de Chrismate* & *de ablutione pedum.*
17. In the *Council of Sardica*, the *3rd, 4th,* and *5th canons* are forged.
18. In the *Council of Nice*, all save 20 are forged.
19. Certain Roman Councils under Sylvester are forged. For he was at this time dead, and therefore could not confirm them. *Zozom. lib* 2.
20. To the *sixth canon of the Council of Nice* are patched these words, "That the Roman Church has always had the supremacy."
21. Lastly, I will not omit that Pope Sozimus, Bonifacius, and Caelestinus, falsified the *canons of the Council of Nice*, to prove appeals from all places to Rome; so as the bishops of Africa were forced to send for the true copies of the said Council from Constantinople and the churches of Greece.

I might here rehearse many other sins which with the former call for vengeance upon the Roman church, but it shall suffice to have named a few of the principal.

Now in this reason, our Savior Christ prescribes another main duty to His own people: and that is to be careful to eschew all the sins of the Church of Rome, that they may withal escape her deserved plagues and punishments. And from this prescribed duty I observe two things: The first is that every good servant of God must carefully avoid contracts of marriage with professed papists, that is, with such as hold the pope for their head and believe the doctrine of the Council of Trent. For in such matches men hardly keep faith and good conscience, and hardly avoid communication with the sins of the Roman church. A further ground of this doctrine I thus propound: In God's Word there is mentioned a double league between man and man, country and country. The first is the *league of concord*, when one kingdom binds itself to live in peace with another for the maintenance of traffic without disturbance. And this kind of league may stand between God's church and the enemies thereof. The second is the *league of amity*, which is when men, people, or countries bind themselves to defend each other in all causes, and to make the wars of the one the wars of the other. And this league may not be made with those that be enemies of God. Jehoshaphat, otherwise a good king, made this kind of league with Ahab and is therefore reproved by the prophet, saying, "Wouldest thou help the wicked, and love them that hate the Lord?" (2 Chron. 19:2). Now the marriages of Protestants with papists are private leagues of amity between person and person, and therefore not to be allowed. Again, [the Lord says,][23] "Judah hath defiled the holiness of the Lord which he loved, and hath married the daughters of a strange

23. The 1635 edition does not include the words, *the Lord says*.

god" (Mal. 2:11), where is flatly condemned marriages made with the people of a false god. Now the papists by the consequents of their doctrine and religion turn the true Jehovah into an idol of their own brain, as I have showed, and the true Christ revealed in the written Word into a feigned "christ" made of bread. Yet if such a marriage be once made and finished, it may not be dissolved. For such parties sin not simply in that they marry, but because they marry not in the Lord, being of divers religions. The fault is not in the substance of marriage, but in the manner of making it. And for this cause the apostle commands the believing party not to forsake or refuse the unbelieving party, being a very infidel (which no papist is) if he or she will abide [1 Cor. 7:13].

The second thing is that every servant of God must take heed how he travels into such countries where popish religion is established lest he partake in the sins and punishments thereof. Indeed, to go upon ambassage[24] to any place, or to travel for this end, that we may perform the necessary duties for our special or general callings, is not unlawful. But to travel out of the precincts of the church only for pleasure's sake and to see strange fashions has no warrant. And hence it is, that many men which go forth in good order well minded, come home with crazed consciences. The best traveler of all is he that—living at home or abroad—can go out of himself and depart from his own sins and corruptions by true repentance.

24. *Ambassage*: embassy.

ADVERTISEMENT TO ALL FAVORERS OF THE ROMAN RELIGION

Showing that the Said Religion is Against the Catholic Principles and Grounds of the Catechism.

Great is the number of them that embrace the religion of the present Church of Rome, being deceived by the glorious title of universality, antiquity, succession. And no doubt, though some be willfully blinded, yet many devoted this way never saw any other truth. Now of them and the rest I desire this favor, that they will but weigh and ponder with themselves this one thing, which I will now offer to their considerations, and that is, "That the Roman religion now established by the Council of Trent, is in the principal points thereof against the very grounds of the Catechism *that have been agreed upon ever since the days of the apostles, by all churches.*" These grounds are four: the first is, the Apostles' Creed; the second is, the Decalogue, or Ten Commandments; the third is, the form of prayer called the Lord's Prayer; the fourth is, the Institution of the two sacraments, baptism and the Lord's Supper [1 Cor. 11:23].

That I may in some order manifest this which I say, I will begin with the symbol or creed:

And first of all it must be considered that some of the principal doctrines believed in the Church of Rome are, that the pope or bishop of Rome is the vicar of Christ and the head of the catholic church; that there is a fire of purgatory after this life; that images of God and saints are to be placed in churches and worshipped; that prayer is to be made to saints departed and their intercession to be required; that there is a propitiatory sacrifice daily offered in the mass for the sins of the quick and the dead. These points are of that moment, that without them the Roman religion cannot stand. And in the Council of Trent the curse *anathema* is pronounced upon all such as deny these or any of them. And yet mark: the Apostles' Creed, which has been thought to contain all necessary points in religion to be believed—and has therefore been called the key and rule of faith—this creed, I say, has not any of these points, nor the expositions made thereof by the ancient fathers, nor any other creed or confession of faith made by any council or church for the space of many hundred years. This a plain proof to any indifferent man that these be new articles of faith never known in the apostolic church, and that the fathers and councils could not find any such articles of faith in the books of the Old and New Testament. Answer is made, that all these points of doctrine are believed under the articles, "I believe the catholic church," the meaning whereof they will have to be this, "I believe all things which the catholic church holds and teaches to be believed." If this be as they say, we must needs believe in the church, that is, put our confidence in the church for the manifestation and the certainty of all doctrines necessary to salvation. And thus, the eternal truth of God the Creator shall depend on the determination of the creature; and the written Word of God in this respect is made insufficient, as though it had not plainly revealed all points of doctrine pertaining to salvation. And the ancient churches have been far overseen, that did not propound the former points to be believed as articles of faith but left them to these latter times.

In this creed, *to believe in God* and *to believe the church* are distinguished. *To believe in* is pertaining to the Creator; *to believe*, to the creature. As Ruffinus has noted, when he says, that by this proposition *in*, the Creator is distinguished from the creature, and things pertaining to God from things pertaining to men.[1] And Augustine says, "It must be known that we must believe the church, and *not believe in the church*; because the church is not God, but the house of God."[2] Hence it follows that we must not believe in the saints, nor put our confidence in our works, as the learned papists teach.[3] Therefore Eusebius says, "We ought of right to believe Peter and Paul, but to *believe in* Peter and Paul, that is, to give to the servant the honor of the Lord, we ought not."[4] And Cyprian says, "He does not believe in God, which does not place in Him alone the trust of his whole felicity."[5]

The article, *conceived by the Holy Ghost*, is overturned by the transubstantiation of bread and wine in the mass, into the body and blood of Christ. For here we are taught to confess the true and perpetual incarnation of Christ, beginning in His conception, and never ending afterward. And we acknowledge the truth of His manhood, and that His body has the essential properties of a true body, standing of flesh and bone; having quantity, figure, dimensions—namely length, breadth, thickness; having part out of part—as head out of feet, and feet out of head—being also circumscribed,

---

1. In the margin: Ruff. in Symb.
2. In the margin: *Serm.* 131. *de Temp.*
3. In the margin: *Rhem. Test.* on Rom. 10:14.
4. In the margin: *Euseb. Emiss. hom.* 2. *de Symb.*
5. In the margin: *Cypr. de dupl. Martyr.*

visible, touchable. In a word, it has all things in it, which by order of creation, belong to a body. It will be said that the body of Christ may remain a true body and yet be altered in respect of some quality, as namely circumscription. But I say again, that local circumscription can no way be severed from a body, it remaining a body. For to be circumscribed in place, is an essential property of every quantity; and quantity is the common essence of every body. And therefore, a body in respect of his quantity must needs be circumscribed in one place. This was the judgment of Leo when he said, "The body of Christ is by no means out of the truth of our body."[6] And Augustine, when he said, "*Only* God in Christ so comes, that he does not depart; so returns, that he does not leave us; but man according to body is in place, and goes out of the same place, and when he shall come unto another place, *he is not in that place whence he comes*."[7] To help the matter, they use to distinguish thus: Christ's body in respect of the whole essence thereof may be in many places; but not in respect of the whole quantity, whereby it is only in one place;[8] but as I have said, they speak contraries, for quantity (by all learning) is the essence of a body, without which a body cannot be.

In the creed we confess that Christ is ascended into heaven, and there after His ascension sits at the right hand of His Father, and that according to His manhood. Hence, I conclude, that Christ's body is not really and locally in the sacrament, and in every host, which the priest consecrates. This argument was good when Vigilius against Eutyches said, "When it (the flesh) was on earth, it was not in heaven; and because it is now in heaven, it is not on earth."[9] And he adds afterward, that this is the catholic

6. In the margin: *Epist.* 70.

7. In the margin: *Tract.* 31. *in Ioh.*

8. In the margin: *Totalitate essentiae, non totalitate quantitatis.*

9. In the margin: *Lib.* 4.

faith and confession. And it was good when Fulgentius said, "According to His human substance He was absent from earth, when He was in heaven, and He left the earth when He ascended into heaven." And, "the same inseparable Christ, according to His whole manhood *leaving the earth*, locally ascended into heaven, and sits at the right hand, and according to the same whole manhood He is to come to judgment."[10] And it was good when Cyril said, "No man doubts but that when He ascended into heaven, though He be always present by the power of His Spirit, *He was absent in respect of the presence of His flesh*."[11] And it was good when Augustine said, "According to the flesh which the Word assumed, He ascended into heaven; *He is not here*. There He sits at the right hand of the Father; and He is here according to the presence of His majesty." And, "He went as He was man, and He abode as He was God; He *went by that whereby He was in one place*; He *abode* by that whereby He was everywhere."

Again, in that we believe the catholic church, it follows that the catholic church is invisible, because things seen are not believed. And the answer commonly used, that we believe the holiness of the church, will not serve the turn. For the words are plain, and in them we make confession, that we believe not only the holiness of the church, but also the church itself.

Lastly, the articles remission of sins, resurrection of the body, and life everlasting, contain a confession of special faith. For the meaning of them is thus much: I believe the remission of my own sins, and the resurrection of my own body to life everlasting, and that by the judgment of learned antiquity. Augustine says, "If you also believe that *you shall rise again* and ascend into heaven (because you are sure of so great a patron), you are certain of

---

10. In the margin: *Ad Thras.*

11. In the margin: *Cyril l.* 9. *in Ioh.*

so great a gift."[12] And, "Make not Christ less, *who brings you* to the kingdom of heaven, for remission of sins. Without this faith, if any come to baptism, he shuts the gate of mercy against himself." And, "Whosoever faithfully believes, and holds this profession of his faith (in which all his sins *are forgiven him*) let him prepare his will to the will of God, and not fear his passage by death."[13] And, "The whole sacrament of baptism stands in this, that we believe the resurrection of the body and remission of sins *to be given us* of God." And, "He gave these keys to the church—that whosoever in His church, should not believe his sins to be forgiven, they should not be forgiven unto him; and whosoever believed, and turned from them, abiding in the lap of the said church, at length shall be healed by faith and amendment of life."[14] And, "That which you have heard to be fulfilled in the glorious resurrection of Christ, believe that the very *same shall be fulfilled in you*, in the last judgment, and the resurrection of your flesh, shall restore you for all eternity. For unless you shall believe that *you are* to be repaired by death, you cannot come to the reward of life eternal."[15] And in ancient time, the article of the resurrection has been rehearsed on this manner, *The resurrection of this flesh*, and the last applied unto it, *To everlasting life*.[16] Hence then two main opinions of the Church of Rome are quite overthrown: one, that we cannot by special faith be certain of the remission of our sins, and the salvation of our souls; the other, that a man truly justified may fall away and be damned. Now this

---

12. In the margin: *Symb. ad Catech. lib.* 4 *c.* 7 & *l.* 2. *c.* 10.

13. In the margin: *Serm.* 115. *de Temp.*

14. In the margin: *De Doct. Christ. l.* 1. *cap.*18.

15. In the margin: *Serm.* 123. *de Temp.*

16. In the margin: *Ruffin. in Symb. Aug. de Symb. l.* 1 *c.* 6 *ad Catech. &* *Enchir. c.* 44.

cannot be, if the practice of the ancient church be good which has taught us to believe everlasting life jointly with remission of sins.

To come to the Decalogue:[17]

First of all it is a rule in expounding the several commandments that where any vice is forbidden, there the contrary virtue is commanded—and all virtues of the same kind, with all their causes, occasions, furtherance. This rule is granted of all; and hence it follows that counsels of perfections, if they have in them any furtherance of virtue, are enjoined in and by the law, and therefore prescribe no state of perfection beyond the scope of the law.

Second, the commandment, "Thou shalt not make to thyself any graven image, etc." has two separate parts: The first forbids the making of carved or graven images. The second forbids the adoration of them. Now the first part is notably expounded by Moses, "Take good heed unto yourselves, that ye corrupt not yourselves and make you a graven image or representation of any figure in the likeness of male or female" (Deut. 4:16). Mark the reason of this prohibition in the same place: "For," says he, "ye saw no image in the day the Lord spake unto you in Horeb," and, "Ye heard the voice of the words, but saw no similitude save a voice" (v. 12). Now the reason being understood of the image of God Himself, the prohibition must needs be understood. Again, there is no question that God directs His commandment against a sin in speculation, but against some common and wicked practice of the Jews, and that was to represent God Himself in likenesses and bodily forms [Isa. 40:18]. And that was also the practice of the Gentiles, that were more gross in this kind than the Jews [Rom. 1:23]. This then is plain to any indifferent man, that the first part of the commandment forbids the making of graven images or likenesses of the true Jehovah; and thus the Roman

17. This paragraph break is not in the original.

catechism understands the words. As for the second part, it must be understood according to the meaning of the first; and therefore, it forbids us to bow down to any image of God. Hence then it follows that to worship God or saints in, or at images, and to worship images with religious worship, is abominable idolatry. And common reason might teach us thus much. For they that adore and worship the true God in images do bind the presence of God—His operation, grace, and His hearing of us—to certain things, places, [and] signs to which He has not bound Himself, either by commandment or promise. And this is otherwise to worship God—and to seek for His blessings—than He has commanded Himself to be worshipped, or promised to hear us. Upon this ground is plainly overthrown the excuse which they make, that they worship not images but God and saints in images; for neither God nor the saints do acknowledge this kind of honor, but they abhor it. Whence it follows necessarily, that they worship nothing beside the image, or the device of their own brain, in which they feign to themselves such a God as will be worshipped and receive our prayers at images. It will be said that the papists do not otherwise tie the worship and invocation of God to images than God tied Himself to the sanctuary and the temple of Solomon. And I say again, it was the will of God that He would show His presence and be worshipped at the sanctuary, and the Jews had the warrant of God's Word for it. But we have no like warrant—either by promise or commandment—to tie God's presence to an image or crucifix. Again, reason yet further may discover their idolatry. They, which worship they know not what, worship an idol; but the papists worship they know not what. I prove it thus: To the consecration of the host, there is required the intention of the priest, at the least virtually, as they say. And if this be true, it follows that none of them can come to the mass or pray in faith, but he must always doubt of that which is lifted up by the hands of the priest in the mass, whether it be bread or the body and blood of Christ. For none can have any certainty of the intention of the priest in consecrating this bread and this wine, but rather may have a just occasion of doubting, by reason of the common ignorance and looseness of life in such persons.

Third, the commandment touching the Sabbath gives a liberty to work six days in the ordinary affairs of our callings—and this liberty cannot be repealed by any creature. The Church of Rome therefore errs, in that it prescribes set and ordinary festival days, not only to God, but also to saints—enjoining them as straitly and with as much solemnity to be observed as the Sabbath of the Lord.

Fourth, the fifth commandment, or (as they say) the fourth, enjoins children to obey father and mother in all things, especially in matters of moment, as in their marriage and choice of their callings, and that even to death. And yet the Church of Rome, against the intent of this commandment, allows that clandestine marriages, and the vow of religion, shall be in force, though they be without and against the consent of wise and careful parents.

Fifth, the last commandment of lust forbids the first motions to sin that are before consent. I prove it thus: Lusting is forbidden in the former commandments as well as in the last; yes, lusting that is joined with consent. As in the commandment, "Thou shalt not commit adultery," is forbidden lusting after our neighbor's wife; and in the next, lusting after our neighbor's goods, etc. Now if the last commandment also forbid no more but lust with consent, it is confounded with the rest. And by this means there shall not be ten distinct words, or commandments, which to say is absurd. It remains therefore that the lust here forbidden goes before consent. Again, the philosophers knew that lust with consent was evil, even by the light of nature. But Paul, a learned Pharisee, and therefore more than a philosopher, knew not lust to be sin that is forbidden in this commandment [Rom. 7:7]. Lust therefore that is forbidden here, is without consent. Wicked then is the doctrine of the Roman church, teaching that "in every mortal sin is required an act commanded of the will." And hence they say, "Many thoughts against faith and unclean imaginations are no sins."[18]

Lastly, the words of the second commandment, "and show mercy to thousands of them that love me and keep my commandments," overthrows all human merits. For if the reward be given of mercy to them that keep the law, it is not given for the merit of the work done.

To come to the third part of the Catechism: The Lord's Prayer is a most absolute and perfect form of prayer. For which cause it was called of Tertullian, "The breviary of the gospel." And Caelestinus says, "The law of praying is the law of believing, and the law of working."[19]

Now in this prayer we are taught to direct our prayers to God alone, "Our Father, etc.," and that only in the name and mediation of Christ. For God is our Father only by Christ. It is needless therefore, to use any invocation of saints, or to make them our mediators of intercession unto God. And it is sufficient if we pray only unto God in the name of Christ alone.

In the fourth petition, we say thus, "Give us our daily bread." In which words, we acknowledge that every morsel of bread is the mere gift of God. What madness then is it for us to think that we should merit the kingdom of heaven by works, that cannot merit so much as bread?

In the next petition, "Forgive us our debts," four opinions of the Roman religion are directly overthrown: The first is, concerning human satisfactions. For the child of God is here, after his conversion, taught to humble himself day by day, and to pray

18. In the margin: *Mol. tract. c.* 27 *conc.* 4.

19. This paragraph break is not in the original.

for the pardon of his daily sins. Now to make satisfaction and to sue for pardon be contrary. The second opinion here overthrown is touching merits. For we do acknowledge ourselves to be debtors unto God, yes bankrupts. And that beside the main sum of many thousand talents, we daily increase the debt, therefore we cannot possibly merit any of the blessings of God. It is mere madness to think that they which cannot pay their debts, but rather increase them day by day, should deserve or purchase any of the goods of the creditors, or the pardon of their debts. And if any favor [is] showed them, it comes of mere goodwill without the least desert. In a word, this must be thought upon, that if all we can do will not keep us from increasing the main sum of our debt, much less shall we be able by any merit to diminish the same. By good right therefore do all the servants of God cast down themselves and pray, "Forgive us our debts." The third opinion is that punishment may be retained, the fault being wholly remitted. But this cannot stand, for here sin is called our debt. Because by nature we owe unto God obedience, and for the defect of this payment, we further owe unto Him the forfeiture of punishment. Sin then is called our debt in respect of the punishment. And therefore, when we pray for the pardon of sin, we require the pardon not only of fault, but of the whole punishment. And when a debt is pardoned, it is absurd to think that the least payment would remain. The fourth opinion is that a man in this life may fulfill the law, whereas in this place every servant of God is taught to ask a daily pardon for the breach of the law. Answer is made that our daily sins are venial and not *against the law*, but *beside the law*. But this which they say is against the petition; for a debt that comes by forfeiture is against the bond or obligation. Now every sin is a debt causing the forfeiture of punishment, and therefore is not beside—but directly against—the law.

In this clause, "as we forgive our debtors," it is taken for granted that we may certainly know that we are in love and charity with men, when we make reconciliation. Why then may not we know certainly that we repent and believe and are reconciled to God, which all Roman Catholics deny?

In the last words, "and lead us not into temptation," we pray not that God should free us from temptation—for it is otherwhiles good to be tempted [Ps. 26:1]—but that we be not left to the malice of Satan and held captive of the temptation. For here, *to be led into temptation*, and *to be delivered*, are opposed. Now hence I gather, that he which is the child of God truly justified and sanctified, shall never fall wholly and finally from the grace of God. And I conclude on this manner: That which we ask according to the will of God shall be granted. But this the child of God asks: that he might never be wholly forsaken of his Father and left captive in temptation [1 John 5:14]. This therefore shall be granted.

This clause, "Amen," signifies a special faith touching all the former petitions, that they shall be granted, and therefore a special faith concerning remission of sins, which the Roman church denies.

To come to the last place, to the institution of the sacrament of the Lord's Supper [1 Cor. 11:23]:[20]

1. In which, first of all, the real presence is by many circumstances overthrown. Out of the words, "he took and brake," it is plain that [that] which Christ took was not His body, because He cannot be said with His own hands to have taken, held, and broken Himself—but the very bread. 2. Again, Christ said not, "under the form of bread," or "in bread," but "This," that is, "bread is my body." 3. Bread was not given for us, but only the body [of] Christ. And in this first institution, the body of Christ was not really given

20. This paragraph break is not in the original.

to death. 4. The cup "is the New Testament" by a figure; why may not the bread be the body of Christ by a figure also?

5. Christ did eat the supper but not Himself. 6. We are bidden to do it "till He come." Christ then is not bodily present. 7. Christ bids the bread to be eaten "in a remembrance of Him," but signs of remembrance are of things absent.

8. If the popish real presence be granted, then the body and blood of Christ are either severed or joined together. If severed, then Christ is still crucified. If joined together, then the bread is both the body and blood of Christ; whereas the institution says, "The bread is the body, and the wine is the blood."

2. Again, here is condemned the administration of the sacrament under one only kind. For the commandment of Christ is, "Drink ye all of this" (Matt. 26:27). And this commandment is rehearsed to the church of Corinth in these words, "Do this as oft as ye drink it in remembrance of me" (1 Cor. 11:25). And no power can reverse this commandment, because it was established by the sovereign head of the church.

These few lines, as also the former treatise, I offer to the view and reading of them that favor the Roman religion—willing them with patience to consider this one thing, that their religion, if it were catholic and apostolic (as they pretend), could not be contrary so much as in one point, to the grounds of all catechisms that have been used in churches confessing the name of Christ ever since the apostles' days. And whereas it crosses the said grounds in sundry points of doctrine (as I have proved), it is a plain argument that the present Roman religion is degenerate. I write not this despising or hating their persons for their religion, but wishing unfeignedly their conversion in this world, and their salvation in the world to come.

FINIS.

Made in the USA
Middletown, DE
06 July 2024

56755852R00144